KELSO'S SHRUG BOOK

KELSO'S SHRUG BOOK

by PAUL KELSO

HATS
OFF™

Published by Hats Off Books™
610 East Delano Street, Suite 104
Tucson, Arizona 85705
ISBN: 1-58736-116-7
LCCN: 2002093086
Book design by Summer Mullins.

Cover illustration by Stephen Wedan. "Dylan," 10x16 inches, pencil. Steve is an artist and writer
who lives in Virginia with his wife, three children, and dog. He can be contacted at swedan@erols.com.

BRINGING IT UP TO DATE

"When is Kelso's shrug book gonna be available?"

People were asking the question, and I know a title when I see one. But why do we need a book, you ask? Every weight trainer knows how to shrug, right? Don't bet on it. I've been teaching and writing about my training ideas for over three decades, but for readers coming across them for the first time, here is what you are going to get:

I'll take you through a couple dozen different ways to shrug and how to use these variations to strengthen the shoulder girdle and to improve your physique, competitive lifts, and stages within lifts. "New" shrugs are included that I have not published before.

All the shrug information from my previous articles and books is surveyed and presented, plus new chapters and developments, ideas from others, and some revisions in my thinking. Photos illustrating the exercises are included with each chapter. Rather than professionally produced photos with a high-priced model I have chosen pics of trainees, friends, and lifters who volunteered their shots. Real people.

This is not a scientific treatise and I have tried to keep the explanations simple. The next paragraph is about as high-toned as I get:

Rather than some kind of magical single exercise, "Kelso" shrugs are the application of a principle of training for the shoulder girdle and upper torso based on the natural adduction and retraction of the scapulae (the shrugging motion) and the many ranges of movement possible. Sounds complicated? Actually, it's easy once you get the hang of it.

The "shrug principle" is applied here to a number of exercise movements and muscle groups, specifically for strength training, competitive lifting, and bodybuilding. They may be used for any number of purposes. Everyone who has given the methods a fair trial in the past knows they work, although results do vary from person to person.

An entire chapter is devoted to "shrugs" for improving the bench press and another for the other competitive lifts. Specific techniques are presented for strengthening the "*lateral arch*" in the bench press. Perhaps I am best known as a powerlifting writer, but many "shrug" exercises in this book also have bodybuilding applications new to most readers.

The book is rounded out with training info for "trap bars" and other such bars now on the market that feature parallel and other grip capability, and an expanded section on ribcage expansion and weight gain.

It isn't really accurate to talk about a "Kelso" shrug in the same way as a "Hack" lift, a "Zercher" squat, or a "Hise" shrug. Those lifts are individual and named for men who either invented the movements or became so proficient in their use that the lift is still identified with them. I simply experimented with and wrote about shrugs of all kinds. I came up with many of the shrug movements in this book on my own, only to discover later that someone else had beat me to them long before. If my name has become attached to any movements in this book it's because I keep hollering about how well they work and attempting to get the word out.

Any time over the years I thought I had cornered every possible type of "shrug," somebody would come up with a new one or I'd discover a variation in an article by an old timer in a seventy-five-year-old magazine. For that reason, I have greatly expanded my former writings. Also, a few workout programs for using the shrugs and other techniques in your regular training will be found in the appendix. How I got hooked on shrug variations is traced in the first chapter.

I have included some history and the names of many people who experimented with or used shrugs over the years. I wish all iron game writers would take this approach for three reasons: 1) because iron game history is fascinating, 2) to protect new trainees from misinformation, and 3) to give credit where it is due.

More than half a dozen variations of the "trap bar," with their own patented features and trademarked names, are now on the market. The basics in chapter five work fine with any of them. To avoid confusion, I will refer in this book to all such bars as "trap bars" *generically*, while giving credit to Al Gerard for the name and the device known as the Gerard Trap Bar that started the parallel grip deadlift craze. (In fact, patents for such bars were applied for before the Gerard model came along, but the earlier versions were never widely produced or never caught on with trainees and died out.) I do not recommend one bar over another, as that is a choice for the trainee.

There is a dispute about why—or how well—the ribcage enhancement ideas work as presented in chapter six. The nay-sayers insist that no one much over twenty three years old can expect any changes in bone structure, specifically ribcage expansion, because the bones become "set" around that age. Actually, *this type of training is not really about bones*, but I'll present arguments from both sides.

The Kelso Shrug Course and *The Bone Structure and Growth Course* were fully copyrighted in 1981. *The Kelso Shrug System* book (now out of print) was compiled after I came to Japan in 1989, and published by Middle Coast in 1993. Iron Mind Enterprises, Inc., published another of my books, *Powerlifting Basics: Texas-Style*, in 1996.

I now teach English at a Japanese university. I live north of Tokyo and married Sumiko in 1997. She was Tochigi state powerlifting champ at 56 kg two years running, and ranked fifth in Japan in her Masters age group. I'm still training at age sixty-five.

I remain active in the game, having sent back close to forty articles and meet reports from Asia to magazines like *Powerlifting USA, Hardgainer,* and *Iron Man*, including coverage of five Asian powerlifting championships, two IPF Worlds and the 2001 World Games. I have written over eighty weights-related articles, all told since 1984. See the list of articles related to this book in the appendix.

I've had a heckuva time during my fifty years in the iron game. It has carried me across the United States, to Thailand, the Philippines, Taiwan, Korea, and all over Japan. I have made wonderful friends wherever I have flung down my gym bag.

But best of all is still the occasional letter from a trainee who writes to tell me of his or her success with my methods. I look forward to hearing from all of you or reading in one of the mags of your great day in competition.

Paul Kelso, April 2002
Utsunomiya City, Japan

TABLE OF CONTENTS

Backgrounds and training for general growth and competition powerlifting. Suggested courses.

Specific exercises for expanding the ribcage and stimulating growth. Controversies about this method and heel height in squatting examined.

CHAPTER ONE

A SHRUGGER'S EDUCATION

Over the last two decades you may have seen articles I've written for the magazines about "Kelso Shrugs." Sometimes they are mentioned on weight-game Internet forums. Those who have seriously practiced these techniques report success. But for many the question remains: What the heck is a Kelso Shrug and who or what is a Kelso?

In the first place, *the Kelso Shrug is not a single exotic exercise, but rather a training <u>principle</u> based on the natural adduction and retraction of the scapulae (the shrugging motion) and the various ranges of movement of the entire shoulder girdle.* These natural movements may be applied with resistance for different purposes using a wide variety of equipment.

I know that's a jawbreaker, so I'm going to explain it as we go along.

I applied this natural range of movement of the scapulae and shoulder girdle to a number of exercises, lifts, and stages within lifts, and tried my ideas out on every piece of gym equipment I could find. I found that by varying angles of attack, hand spacing, and grips, contractions in different muscle groups could be directed and concentrated.

The second part of the question is easy to answer. I've been hanging around weight rooms since the early 1950s as a trainee, competitor, coach, and correspondent. I am not a famous champion, just one of the millions of guys who loves weight sports. At age sixteen, I was very slender, had a narrow chest measuring 38 inches, weighed 154 pounds, and stood 5'10". When I went in the Army three years later, I weighed 196 pounds at 6'1", so I was doing something right. (I eventually topped out at 6'2" and 226 in shape). My training consisted of the "Olympic" lifts, high-rep squat programs, and wrestling workouts. Powerlifting didn't get going until the mid-60s.

In 1954-55 I was lucky to train with future national heavyweight weightlifting champion Sid Henry (who had been a year or two ahead of me in high school) and Bill and Linwood Gilliland, perennial Texas champions. On the pro wrestling side, I pounded the mat with Ray Gunkel, huge Hugh "Tex" McKenzie, and character actor

Tarzan Mike Lane, who played the Primo Carnera role opposite Humphrey Bogart in the Budd Schulberg movie "The Harder They Fall."

These men were light-years ahead of me in strength and ability but possessed a quality that has been shunted aside by the commercialism that now infests our game. They felt they had an obligation to help the new kids on their way up. They received little but personal satisfaction from doing so. I'm not the only "old timer" who laments the passing of the tradition of giving something back.

I wrote the shrug system book in 1991-92. I was 54 at the time, weighed 220, did not have a beer gut and my muscles had not turned to fat. Today I am 65, weigh around 230 when more or less in shape, and still train as often as I can. My chest measurement varies around 48-50" depending on my weight. I actually gained ten pounds of muscle in my middle fifties. Don't let anyone tell you that can't be done.

Over the years I have been a soldier, a folksinger, a seller of fishing tackle, a newspaperman, a teacher, and a historian. None of that put an inch on my arm.

Who I am is easy to answer. What the Kelso shrug principle is requires a little more explanation.

Anyone who has been weight training for any length of time soon learns what a "shrug" is. It is standing upright with a bar or dumbbells hanging at arms' length and trying to touch the ears with the shoulders. What is not widely known is that there are dozens of possible variations for a variety of purposes.

I know it might seem presumptuous to name a training principle after oneself, but it does have to be identifiable. When I began experimenting with shrug styles in the early sixties (I offered the original *Kelso Shrug Course* back in 1981), I had never seen most of the movements I included published anywhere previously, except for the standing shrug and the Hise shrug. This doesn't mean no one else ever thought of them, they were just never gathered together and codified into a system by a fanatic shrugger like myself.

In fact, *Flex* magazine ran an article in 1986, under the name of first Mr. Olympia Larry Scott, suggesting that some of the shrug variations I had advocated in an earlier *Iron Man* piece had been practiced by famous names long dead. That didn't surprise me at all. In 1987, the publication's sister magazine ran an article by bodybuilding writer Bill Dobbins, who claimed scapular retractions for the lats, and lower and middle traps had *occurred* to him while using a seated rowing machine. Never mind that these movements likely had been around longer than the fifty years the publisher claimed to have been training champions.

Since I began writing on the subject, other names for the exercises have appeared, which do not bother me at all, such as "rearward shrugs," "incline shrugs," "serratus shrugs," and more. Even "Dr. Squat" Fred Hatfield has said that in years past he invented and wrote about the exercise I call the Lat Shrug. I first wrote about it in 1968.

I am willing to bet it was around long before that, but haven't found it anywhere in the literature, and believe me, I've tried.

Who invented what when is pretty much irrelevant. What does surprise me—and bothers me—is that these techniques and movements were not better known long ago and are not in more general use today. They are as obvious to me as the dumbbell curl.

In this book you will meet a number of men who have used different types of shrugs for different reasons. I'm sure many of these shrugs go back to the beginnings of modern physical culture in the nineteenth century. Little is really new in weight training. Heck, there is a 2,000-year old mosaic wall mural in a lava-buried spa in Pompeii, Italy, showing a guy in a short skirt using dumbbells!

I was tall, lanky, and big-boned as a kid, with a hollow between my shoulder blades big enough to hide a football in. I did power cleans and bent over rows for a couple of years and developed some lats and upper traps, as well as a pretty good pull for Olympic style lifts, but I still had protruding scapulae and a knobby backbone between.

One day I rather carelessly bent over to move a bar out of my way, and sort of heaved it or shrugged it aside. I felt a sharp response in my lower traps. Then I picked up the bar in a bent over rowing stance and "shrugged" it again. Same response. I spent the rest of that workout doing bent over shrugs with overhand, underhand, and varied wide and narrow hand spacing. I felt a different muscle response with each change of grip.

I didn't shout "Eureka!" or feel like I had just found the Holy Grail, but I knew I was on to something. The hollow between my shoulder blades is long since gone. I discovered over the years that I could utilize the shrug principle in any position that I could get my upper body into, and even developed some negative applications as well.

Let's get started. Please refer to the glossary (Appendix III) if unfamiliar with any of the terms used.

Lat Shrug or "Kelso" Shrug, bent over: Original 1981 drawing, showing possible directions of retraction.

LAT SHRUG

I've read in the mags over the years about champions who practice four to six exercises four to five sets apiece during a back workout. *The problem is that the smaller assisting muscle groups tend to give out before the large muscles you're trying to reach.*

Don't believe it?

The next time you do bent over rows, keep going on the last set until you can't do one more repetition without cheating or getting help from your training partner. Then, without changing position or putting the bar down, start doing the "shrug" movement I call the Lat Shrug. You'll be able to do four or five or more reps before your lats and traps go on strike.

Here we go. Take your position for bent over rowing. Select a weight you can handle for 8-10 reps. Lift the weight from the floor and get a full stretch. Now, without bending your arms, shrug (retract your scapulae) so that the bar rises toward the lower part of your sternum or lower pecs.

Concentrate the contraction on a point between your shoulder blades, not up toward your ears, and preferably even down farther where your lower traps insert. The contraction is focused back and down. *(Keeping the shoulder blades down and back aids the deadlift.)* Lower the bar to stretch and repeat. Using a fairly close, underhand grip will strongly affect the lats as well as the trap area and bring the terres and rhomboids into play.

That last is the style that has become known to many as a "Kelso Shrug," rightly or not. In fact, I have called this movement the Lat Shrug in most magazine articles I've written, although it works not only the lats but many muscles in the upper back.

I first told Peary Rader at *Iron Man* magazine about my shrug ideas in 1967, and he discussed them in his "Reader's Roundup" column. Here's Peary writing in Vol. 28, No. 1, of the October-November, 1968, *Iron Man*, page 42.

> *Paul Kelso sends a new exercise which he says is great for developing the muscles in the upper back across the scapulae or shoulder blades. Here is the way it is performed.*
>
> *Take a bar loaded to about 70 or 80% of your rowing motion poundage and then assume the bent over rowing position, but instead of bending the arms you only shrug the shoulders upward and then roll them slightly backward and finish the movement with an arching of the back. This can become a strenuous exercise if you're not used to it. One variation is to use a close grip with knuckles up; another is with the under grip which affects the rhomboid area; still another is to do a full rotating motion. Paul says that by doing this in combination with rowing, alternating sets as in super setting, it pumps him up so fast that a high number of sets is not possible for him....*
>
> *Paul says this really did the job in thickening his back, an area often neglected by bodybuilders.*

These moves described at that time are slightly different than the movement I laid out above, but they all work. *Adding that back arch at the end of each rep is a killer,* as is super-setting the rows and shrugs, but it makes the exercise more intense.

An overhand grip will give you a more general trap and upper back response with the emphasis on the middle trap area; the underhand grip is more for lower traps and lats. For greater stability and isolation, perform the movement with any style grip on a high-rowing bench, incline bench, or seated rowing machine. This will take the legs and lower back out of the movement and allow the upper back to do the work.

Try the knuckles-up style on an incline bench set at a 45-degree angle or lower. Varying the angle of incline calls different muscles into play, as does changing the focus and direction of the contraction. Using a wide grip can help young trainees structurally on down the stretch. And yes, you can use dumbbells with great results, especially on an incline bench.

Experiment on various pieces of equipment at the gym. You can apply the shrug principle to just about any exercise or piece of equipment calling for use of the arms. For instance, sitting on the floor and leaning way forward toward a low pulley and shrugging back toward the lower lat insertions is excellent, as is using a seated rowing machine while leaning forward or back. You can also use an overhead machine leaning back or forward.

The T-bar rowing machine (a favorite shrugging tool of legendary bench presser Big Jim Williams in the '70s), cable pulleys (overhead or seated), as well as any number of machines, including the cable-crossover apparatus, can be used. Just stand between them and shrug straight in. The lower setting develops the upper areas more while the upper setting affects the middle and lower portions.

Crossover cable shrugs will also help bodybuilders train wide in addition to aiding them in getting the scapulae to semi-dislocate for a greater lat spread or "flair," as the old timers insisted on spelling it. These movements will not only develop the muscles targeted but bodybuilders will be happy to discover they provide fullness up the middle of the back, carve out the line of separation between the upper lat and the lower edge of the shoulder blade, and deepen the line of the lat along the rib cage as seen from the front.

Now let's talk a little about sets and reps.

One way to incorporate these variations into your regular routine is to add a set of shrugs after each of the different exercises you now perform: same grip, same position, no arm pull. You could also cut your total number of sets down and tack on two or three sets of "Kelso" shrugs of your choice. Super-setting a full range of motion row or pull with a shrug variation in the same position is extremely intense and will result in quick congestion of the muscles targeted. Alternating one rep of full range of motion rowing with a rep of Lat Shrug will congest the muscles quickly and to the edge of excruciation.

I find that three sets of shrugs after a general back workout is plenty. Repetition schemes are similar, as for any exercise, but some powerlifters go as high as 5 x 15 with the standing shrug, believing that gives them the best result. A weight that allows only five reps or less per set restricts movement and may lead to injury. Maxing out with single rep shrugs has no purpose, but some do it just for the challenge.

At a West Coast bodybuilding show I attended some years ago, I was struck by the fact that out of the 80-odd entries there were only six or eight examples of what I call great backs. There were maybe a dozen guys who appeared to have ever performed a power clean. I'm talking about that double column of muscle paralleling the spine from the tailbone to the back of the neck and that striking sweep of trapezius muscle from the back of the neck to the rear deltoid, plus visible lower trap development in mid-back.

If you're in need of more bulk and thickness, try the following routine:

Power cleans
Do 3-5 sets of 5 repetitions

One hand dumbbell rows
Do 2-3 sets of 8 repetitions

Lat or "Kelso" Shrugs, bent over, or off an incline bench
Do 2-3 sets of 8 repetitions

The bottom line is that there is no sense in practicing shaping exercises and finishing routines until you have some muscle to shape or finish.

The great thing about the various Kelso-style shrugs is that you can focus the concentration on any spot you wish to work because of the mobility of the scapulae and the angle of attack. It just takes a little practice.

Here are a few tricks. Those who follow pre-exhaustion techniques (see glossary) can use various shrugs before a back exercise and fatigue the target muscles effectively. Stephen Wedan, a respected writer and illustrator for several muscle magazines, and the cover artist of this book, reminded me of another approach years ago. Intensity can be increased by shrugging the scapulae into contraction and *then* continuing the bar movement with arm pull for three inches or so. This method is commonly used by Olympic-style lifters as a timed, sequential part of the pull. The technique could be used with almost any shrug movement in this book, except the Bench Shrug, Shrug Dips, or the Hise Shrug. We'll get to them later on.

Furthermore, this technique has long been known to weight training as the **shrug row** and has been around at least since the 1930s. In 1989, I saw Chester O. Teegarden perform five reps of bent over shrug rows off balks (blocks) with 325 pounds on several occasions, and he was 76 years old! (Chester was a national-class weightlifter in the 1930-40s and defeated the great John Grimek in 1937 at the USA Nationals.) Bill Starr and others have written of the **power shrug**: pulling from the floor or from pins in the rack and continuing the upward path of the bar by shrugging at the top *without* bending the arms. This is done with either snatch or clean width grips and takes practice to learn the timing. It is in wide use among Olympic-style weightlifters. A variant would be to set the traps in the contracted position at the beginning of the lift and keep them there throughout, followed by a slow release to the starting position.

With the **shrug row**, shrug first, then pull. Better look quick, however, as it appears to be one motion. This technique of getting the shoulders back and set before pulling with the arms can be used with most of the shrug variations possible. But because it is very intense, I'm going to go on record as stating that I think the trainee should first practice the straight-arms style for at least.a month or two. (I discuss competitive lifting applications in more detail in chapters three and four.)

I'm warning everybody right now—the variations I'm advocating will work some of your muscles and muscle attachments from angles that have never experienced heavy loads. Start *moderate*, eight to ten rep loads until you have the feel of it. Then build up. Otherwise, you can expect some serious soreness, especially with wide-grip or high-bench isolation.

Poundages: I get a little steamed when I'm in a gym and see somebody doing standing dumbbell shrugs with a pair of 35s and rotating them around like a dowager working on her double chins. A trainee needs to work up to well over bodyweight to achieve any real gains. That is hard to do with a rolling motion.

There is nothing *wrong* with the old standby shrug or with using a rolling motion. The first works the upper traps primarily and the rest of the trapezius secondarily. The rolling motion can be effective as a general moderate weight exercise if you only want to do one movement and to be non-specific, but *specific movements work better*. Some say the rolling motion can lead to injuries. I have never had any problems with it, nor has any one ever reported such to me personally, but I now consider the rolling motion pretty much a waste of time.

I am not an anatomist, but I understand that there are four different muscle bunches that make up the trapezius complex. The variations in this book allow these areas to be attacked specifically.

As we go along, I'll refer to the sport of Weightlifting (which includes the Snatch and the Clean and Jerk) as "Olympic" lifting because the general public often confuses weightlifting with weight training. Most Olympic and power lifters are aware of the truly humongous weights that the top men train with in the shrug; however many budding trainees and most young bodybuilders are not. Top Olympic lifters are able to rep-shrug far more than they can clean, whereas top powerlifters can do reps with weights most of us cannot even deadlift. Many can do sets and reps with more than they can deadlift!

Former Mr. Texas, Dr. Glen Bill Williamz (yes, it's spelled with a 'z'), once performed reps in the standing shrug with 800 pounds at a bodyweight of 220. That is not a misprint. (It was done in a power rack off pins.) Past powerlifting champion John Gamble is reported to have done 780 pounds x 18 reps using straps. So you trainees who are dinking around with upright rows, "face pulls," and close-grip pull downs from overhead, trying to develop some showy little bumps, please give me and yourself a break! Put some weight on the bar and try it my way.

Competitive lifters will find that the practice of the lean forward or face down on an incline shrugs will greatly improve their pull. *By setting the bench at different angles corresponding to stages within the pull, a lifter can attack sticking points.* Working off pins in the power rack is another great way to go. Also important to note is that the use of lifting straps will be of great aid with heavy shrugs.

OK, you say, so what are some of the other variations? How are they performed? I'll sketch out a bunch in the next chapter.

Incline DB Shrug: *Model, Eigi Michibayashi, 75 kg powerlifting champ, Tochigi state, Japan.*

Incline Shrug on machine: *Greg Leistner, strength coach of the new Houstan Texans NFL team, performs "Kelsos" on a Kell t-bar row bench.*

CHAPTER TWO

SHRUG VARIATIONS

The cover blurb says this book is for powerlifters, weightlifters, and bodybuilders. No exercise in these pages is meant to be limited to any of the three groups. The reader should check them all out and pick and choose the movements that suit his purposes.

BENCH SHRUGS

That's right, for the chest: No, I'm not crazy. If the shoulder girdle can move one way under resistance, it can move the other—in short, negative shrugs. Here's a great one for improving the bench press and toughening up the whole upper torso. Take your position for the bench press. Load a weight you can bench for 8-10 reps. Have your training partner hand you the weight and tell him to stay on the job. Now, with the bar at arms' length, shrug (retract) your shoulders back toward the bench and squeeze your scapulae together. Keep your arms straight at all times.

The bar should have dropped a few inches when you crunched the shoulder blades together. Raise the bar up by spreading the scapulae apart and rolling the shoulders up and off the bench. Spread your lats and use your pecs to get your front deltoids moving in towards each other, a sort of a "lat spread" or "lat flair" with resistance. Yes, the old-timers spelled it that way: "flair," not "flare." The bar will rise several inches. Be very careful of the balance, as it can get tricky with the bar held at arms' length. Get off line and the bar could end up in your lap! Always use a spotter for this movement or do it inside a power rack with the lower pins set just below the range of motion. Stuart McRobert, publisher of *Hardgainer* magazine, reports that a "Smith" machine works well with this movement.

I recommend against doing this movement while wearing a bench shirt. The shirt may shift during performance and the lifter may have trouble getting the shoulders back into starting position for the next rep.

Eventually you will be able to work up to huge weights for reps. I have done three reps or more on a good day with more than my best bench press poundage. Some men have reported using 10-15% above their best single bench. But please, work the poundage up over time as you do with any exercise. *Do not use an exaggerated wide grip; you could flirt with shoulder injury or dislocation if you do.*

I used to call this movement the Bench Crunch, as the pecs are strongly contracted at the finish. In the early days of my tinkering I often did this movement with dumbbells and found they allowed a greater range of movement and pectoral contraction than with a bar. However, using a bar allows more weight to be used, and is more specific to the competition lift.

I changed the name of the movement, as it is very much the opposite of the Lat Shrug. Having seen it purloined and referred to as the "Serratus Shrug" in an article in *Muscular Development* the early 1990s, I would agree that it works the serratus as a side benefit. However, it is most effective used with heavy weights to build a powerful shoulder girdle to support big lifts on the bench. Many of the kids on the college team I coached jumped their bench presses up about twenty pounds after a month or two on this exercise.

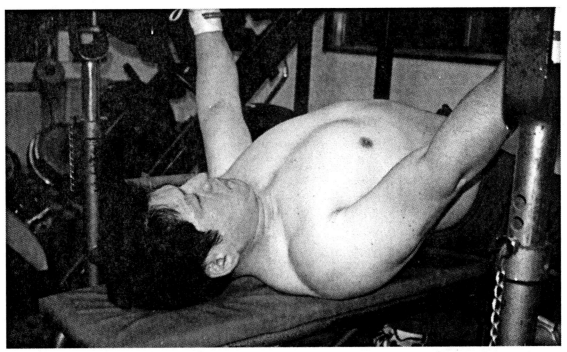

Picture shows retracted position of Bench Shrug with scapulae pinched together at "bottom."

Full extension at "top" of the Bench Shrug. Model—Suguru Uetaki, 100 kg,
Tochigi, Japan, state powerlifting champ.

(By the way, the "Lat Flair" or semi-dislocation of the shoulders blades was a muscle control posing trick used in exhibition by the true old-timer set, and can be seen in their leopard skin leotard photos. Few do it today. You could argue that the word should be "flare" as in "spread," but the old spelling used "flair," referring to "style.")

THE SHRUG DIP

If it's serratus you want, try this: warm up with a set of parallel bar dips. Reassume the starting position and lower the body by allowing your shoulders to rise up toward your ears. Don't bend your arms when lowering your body. Then, raise the body by forcing the shoulders down with pec, lat, lower trap, and serratus contraction. Again, use no arm movement. This shrug dip, coupled with an old Vern Weaver (1963 Mr. America) favorite—straight-arm pull downs on the overhead lat machine—will give you some serratus in a hurry.

I had practiced and written about shrug dips for a number of years when one day I ran into Mister Universe Lance Dreher at Bill Williamz' gym in Tyler, Texas, where Lance was giving a seminar. I described the shrug dip and Lance said he had learned it from Bob Gadja, former Mr. America, in Chicago. Bob called them Monkey Dips.

How these movements have remained largely unknown for so long is beyond me. I consider the shrug dip to be a fine bodybuilding exercise since it also carves out the serratus and lats with delineation. By the way, it is the *direct negative* of the standing shrug with dumbbells or a "trap bar."

Try shrug dips with a dipping belt with some weight on it next time you're feeling masochistic. Leaning forward as if doing Gironda-style dips will put more work on the pecs and complement the decline bench press, while leaning back throws the emphasis on the terres and lats. You can get good results supporting your hands on one bench or on boxes with your feet elevated as if doing triceps dips. Just don't use the arms. An upside down bench shrug or decline effect can be had by "shrugging" in the push-up position.

STANDING SHRUG: REGULAR STYLE

This is the old standby and the most basic, primarily intended to benefit the upper traps, and usually performed with a clean-width grip on a straight bar, dumbbells, "trap bar," or any of the variations of that bar now on the market. The bar is shrugged straight up and lowered under control without rolling the shoulders or pulling to the rear. Great effects can be had with wide hand spacing pulled up toward the ears or to the rear as if finishing a deadlift. Many, including multiple Mr. Olympia winner Lee Haney, did or do the standing shrug with the bar held behind the back. Haney is reported to have used the shrug row technique, pulling two or three inches with the arms in the full contraction stage of the movement.

CHINNING BAR AND OVERHEAD SHRUGS

These involve "shrugging" down the overhead lat bar with scapular action only, or attempting to raise the body with shoulder blade retraction and torso muscle contraction while hanging from a chinning bar. That last is hard to get with. I recommend the trainee start with the overhead pulldown with a very light weight to get the feel of the movement. Doing these from a chinning bar is *tough*, although some people work up to using a loaded weight belt while doing them.

The late Charles A. "There is nothing new in weight training" Smith, who knew everybody and everything in the iron-game and wrote for the Weider magazines for eight years in their early days, once told me that these movements were popular among the old Muscle Beach crowd, and also used by gymnasts.

(See chapter four about overhead shrugs with a bar. This would be a negative of the above, raising and lowering the bar with scapular and shoulder girdle movement.)

CABLE CROSSOVER MACHINE SHRUGS

I've found that doing lat pulldowns or rows "to the side" on a cable crossover machine is extremely good for getting wide, carving out the smaller muscles of the upper back, and developing a "Christmas tree" for bodybuilding purposes. Set the machine on high pulley and stand or kneel in the middle, depending on your height and the angle you want. Using the arms, bending the elbows, pull the handles in toward the body as if trying to touch your elbows together behind the back for several sets.

Then, go *shrug-style*. Take a straight-arm stance and assume a "crucifix" position. Allow a full stretch out to each side until it feels like your shoulder blades are going to pop loose. Then shrug or rotate the scapulae together, trying to pinch them together in the center of your back. Do not bend the elbows during the contraction or the return to the stretch. Do not use any forward or rear lateral motion. Repeat for reps and sets. A word of caution: start light!

These "Lat Flair" shrugs, as I called them in a January 1986 *Iron Man* article, will help bodybuilders and muscle-control practitioners achieve that semi-dislocation the old-timers demonstrated so amazingly.

This movement, and the spring set shrug below, can help in strengthening the "lateral arch" used by competition bench pressers. See chapter three.

Using the low pulley setting on the cable crossover machine has other benefits; see *wide grip shrugs* below.

SPRING SET SHRUG

This shrug is a negative of the above. Remember that spring set exercise where you held the springs behind the back and pressed straight out to each side, rep after rep? Dig that old set out from the bottom of the closet, put some springs on it and stretch it out across the upper back. Press it out to arm's length on each side and then spread the scapulae to force the hands further out and then resist the tension while allowing the scapulae to come together in the middle of your back, without bending the arms. Repeat.

That's right, a "lat spread" with positive and negative resistance.

WIDE GRIP SHRUGS

These movements may be done several ways and are performed with a wide, snatch grip on a straight, Olympic, or power bar and other apparati. In the bent over position, the contraction is to the middle of the back. Standing, to the rear as in finishing a deadlift, works the entire trapezius, while up toward the ears is more upper trap with a strong involvement of the attachments high on the neck. All the wide grip movements aid in widening the shoulder girdle, especially in younger people.

Face down on an incline bench set at any angle works well with the wide grip moves. Resting the forehead on bench or table while in the bent over position will work, but it may stress the neck.

Wide grip work may also be done on the cable crossover machine at either high or low setting or with a long bar on the lat machine set at high or low.

There is an odd result with wide grips: the direction of pull is not back or up as with a "clean" width grip. There is a triangulation from the hands to the focal point of contraction. That causes the muscles to contract in a slightly different direction than usual. I have never been able to properly explain that in words. Try the wide grip. You'll feel what I mean.

Also, an odd result for me with the use of standing wide grip shrugs with a snatch grip on an Olympic bar was the trap development I achieved. I never grew the blocky, ham-butt shaped lumps on either side of the neck so commonly seen. I have a long neck and the wide grip movement and angle of attack affected the trap attachments high on the sides of my neck so that I now have a long slope from neck to shoulder, which in turn makes me look wider. (There may be a scientific basis for this: muscle fibers are believed to become longer when stretched under stress, as it is thought that sarcomeres are added in series to the fibers.)

Wide grip shrugs also carved out delineation between my traps and my sternocleidomastoid as seen from the front and thickened the muscles high on the back of my neck. Body-builders, take note.

Back in the downtown Dallas Y in 1954-55, we had old York sets with the wide ridged rims on the plates. Had the hubs, too. Those plates made for the interesting gripping stunts you can now read about in *Milo* magazine. We would turn the inner 45-pound plates out (the wrong way) so we could grab the bar by the rims and then load on smaller plates. We would deadlift the bar by the rims and then shrug or power-shrug it up a few inches. (Steve Reeves was known to do this – check his trap shape in his photos). It works great but few gyms still have those old plates. If you find any, latch on to them.

HISE BREATHING SHRUG

Joseph Curtis Hise has been called the first powerlifter and the foremost practitioner of the breathing or twenty-rep squat in very abbreviated programs for gaining bulk. You can find his story in many books, so I won't go deeply into it, but during the Great Depression he is reported to have gained 29 pounds of solid weight in *one month* doing little but heavy, high rep squats, behind the neck presses, sleeping, and guzzling milk. The history trail of the Breathing Shrug is a little foggy, but Hise began writing about it in the 1940s or before and the exercise still bears his name.

There are not one but two ways to do this movement, for two different purposes. The first is as Joe Hise applied it—as a breathing movement for the expansion of his rib cage and shoulder girdle, not as a trap builder. The traps will benefit anyway.

You simply shoulder the bar like you are going to squat, inhale, and shrug the bar up toward the ears. The bar is carried in a more or less "high-bar" position, not down the back like in a powerlifter's competition squat. This movement will strengthen the entire shoulder girdle and enhance structural growth. Start with a very moderate squatting weight for a few weeks until you are used to it. Test for the position on your shoulders that allows the most height to be gained. Then pile on the iron, but not so much as to restrict the range of movement. This is a great movement in tandem with 20 rep squats or your deadlift training, especially for relative beginners and intermediates. I suggest 15 or more reps a set, but Hise was known to go as high as 25 reps.

There is an old controversy attached to these movements. It has long been widely believed that high-rep breathing squats, rib-cage stretching exercises, Hise Shrugs, etc., result both in rib cage structure expansion of the chest and shoulder girdle and in stimulating muscular weight gains. I recall reading a theory in *Strength & Health* back in the fifties that they altered the metabolic rate and thus triggered bulk gains, but no one has promoted that possibility lately that I know of.

Certain recent academic studies deny these effects, and the discussion has become something of a schoolyard "Does Too – Does Not" argument. Casey Butt of Canada is working on these matters as I write this (December 2001) and points out that Joe Hise and others of his time believed that the Hise Shrug and its forced breathing resulted in the formation of new rib cartilage and worked many small muscle groups which hold the ribcage in an expanded position. Casey has also come up with a true variation of the Hise Breathing Shrug by holding the bar across the anterior deltoids as if doing front squats. These "*Rack Raises*," as he calls them, allow greater movement and rise in the rib cage than with the bar across the back. (See chapter six.)

I suspect we don't yet fully understand what is happening when these breathing movements are performed. But thousands and thousands of trainees since Hise's time have reported that they do work, and I'm one of the happy practitioners.

Another variation of the Hise Breathing Shrug can be done on a standing calf machine. Try facing the "wrong way" for a really different feel with the movement. However, I have come to believe that the calf machine is an inferior way to do the Hise Shrug. Heavier weights seem to stifle the range of the motion, especially as the arms or yokes that rest on the shoulders press down on the muscles and bone structure more than a bar across your back and even impede breathing. Part of this problem is that machine models vary from gym to gym, angles of leverage differ, and the closer the pads rest to your neck, the worse the discomfort seems to get.

Everybody? Let's use a little common sense here. Some love the calf machine shrug; others hate it and say it's dangerous. But body types and leverages differ from lifter to lifter. Machines differ. If any exercise or technique causes you discomfort or pain, then switch to another one. There are endless exercises to choose from for whatever purpose. As I have written elsewhere, *what works for one, works "on" another.*

The second type of Hise Shrug is a good form of psychological training for heavy squatting and a tremendous power builder when used with lower reps. (See chapter four.)

STERNUM SHRUG

In my article "A Shrugger's Guide," in *Muscular Development*, January, 1989, (the last issue of MD published by York before Twin Labs stepped in), there is a photo of myself and bodybuilding great Arthur Peacock demonstrating a "breathing shrug." The problem is that I didn't explain the movement in the text of the article. I am finally getting around to it.

Take your stance as if you are going to do regular standing shrugs, but with about half the weight you would normally use. Learn the move before you pile the weights back on. The purpose of the exercise is to raise and expand the ribcage and force the sternum up. The secret is in the breathing, which reverses the regular pattern.

Exhale as the bar is shrugged up; inhale as it is lowered. As the bar nears the bottom position, flex the pectorals while rolling your shoulders forward and exhale forcibly, hugging the sides of your chest with the insides of the biceps. Drive the air out of your lungs and force your chest and sternum up!

This shrug can be used along with Rader Chest Pulls, Hise Shrugs, and pullovers for the purpose of bone structure expansion. However, it is *best* used as the finish to the Breathing Stiff-Leg Deadlift as outlined in chapter six.

NEGATIVE SHRUGS

The use of negative resistance movements has become popular in recent years in both strength training and bodybuilding. The Shrug Dip is negative to the action of the conventional standing shrug, as is the Bench Shrug to Lat Shrugs or many movements that forcibly retract the shoulder blades. Overhead shrugs with a bar are negative to Chinning Shrugs (see chapter three). The Spring Set Shrug has an action negative to the Cable Crossover Shrug.

In chapter four, I discuss the *Shrug Hold*, a technique applicable to many movements. A basic use would be to perform conventional standing shrugs in a power rack, using straps, and power-shrug the weight to maximum height and full contraction upward of the shoulder girdle. The weight is held in max contraction position for a count (three to four counts seem to work well) or as long as possible before the bar is lowered under control to the rack pins. Other lifters shrug the traps up into contracted position before starting the rep, and try to hold that position at the top before lowering the bar as slow as possible. Variations of these movements with pre-set traps are sometimes called Starr Shrugs after the well-known lifter and writer Bill Starr.

An exercise that is getting some play as I write these comments (July, 2001) is use of a standing cable row or pulley machine set on low position near the floor. One stands in front of it in a sort of deadlift stance and retracts the scapulae toward the rear as well as up. (I have said before that all kinds of shrug variations are possible on any number of machines or types of apparatus.) This provides continuous tension—positive and negative. A lot of effort is expended maintaining the stance without being pulled forward. That can be good or bad, depending on what you want.

A drawback to the above is that most gym cable machines are "stack" loaded. Almost any intermediate powerlifter or semi-experienced bodybuilder can eventually work up to more weight than the stack in a typical commercial machine has. If they can't, they are not reaching their potential.

One thing I might add to the shrug movements recommended is to try them one hand at a time. This could be useful in correcting an imbalance in development or strength by giving one side of the back or specific area extra work. As I do not presume to advise anyone medically, I will leave any discussion of various shrugs for medical purposes to other, more qualified writers. Paul Chek has written on these subjects.

A word of warning: the trainee should keep the chin up, *with the head erect and not jammed forward* when doing shrugs. This prevents possible upper back nerve damage.

The number of shrugs possible is limited only by your imagination and the variety of equipment available. I'm sure there are other "shrugs" I haven't yet learned about and that guys out there somewhere are tinkering with new ones *right now*. The beauty of these variations is that you can target a specific muscle or area and then zero in on it by adjusting your angle of attack and mentally concentrating the contraction right where you want it.

A course for general strength and growth using some of the above shrugs is listed in Appendix I.

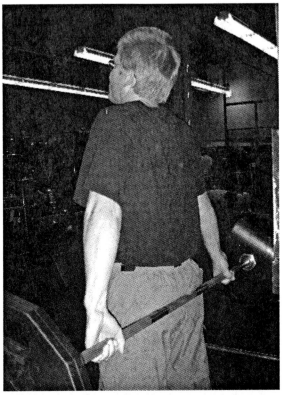

*Pat Henley of Austin, Texas, demonstrates the **Behind Back Shrug**.*

Sternum Shrug. *Mike Bucci of Phoenix, Arizona, finishing a rep by forcing the sternum up.*

Cable Crossover Machine Shrug. *Masatoshi Kashikura, 67.5 kg Tochigi state PL champ, shows the* **extended** *(top) and* **retracted** *(bottom) positions.*

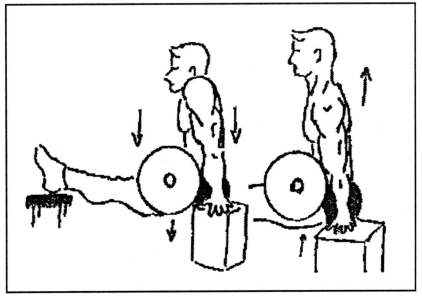

*Variation of the **Shrug Dip**, hands on the bench with feet elevated. Arms are straight; body is raised and lowred with "shrugging" movement. Drawing from the 1981 Shrug Course.*

CHAPTER THREE

SHRUG TRAINING FOR THE BENCH PRESS

Back in the fifties, the common questions among weight men were "How much can you curl?" or "How much can you press?" meaning military-style overhead. The bench press had none of the popularity that it has now that it has become a standard of measuring another's strength. I would still vote for the clean and jerk as a fine indicator of combined strength and athletic ability, but doubt I'd get much support from powerlifters. Some weightlifters and others put down powerlifting, saying it is all brute strength requiring no technique. How wrong they are. Let's get to bench press training and styles and discuss the **"Lateral Arch"** and the concept of the **"Shrug Hold."**

For years magazine articles about the bench concentrated on lockout problems, hand and arm positions, "finding the groove," and so forth. Less has been written about the initial drive off the chest than any other stage of the lift. (Use of bench shirts has modified this equation somewhat; many shirts deliver considerable help getting the bar started off the chest and some super-duper shirts turn the lift into something resembling a lockout.)

Watching top lifters can be revealing. At least two schools of thought about the role of the shoulder girdle in bench pressing are current in the gyms. One is the more traditional style familiar to most trainees, and the other is the exaggerated arching that is becoming very widespread, although not everyone is suited for it. Sivokon of Kazakhstan, who has won seven IPF men's open world championships and five bench press world championships the last time I counted, does not have an exaggerated lower back arch. Japan's benchers won both the men and women's team bench press titles at the world meet in 2001 and exemplify the use of extreme arches in both directions.

There have always been differences in technique and always will be because of the variety of body types and leverages among lifters. The more traditional school might call for lowering the bar to the "high point of the chest" and rotating the elbows out during the lift while the new breed lowers to the upper abs and keeps the elbows in.

We have all seen some lifters who mix the two and have read articles with contradictory opinions.

I do not pretend to be an authority on bench technique, but I do have some ideas for aiding the bench press, whatever the style used.

THE FLARE OR "ROLL" SCHOOL

What is the first thing that happens when the lifter begins to press? Most would say arm drive or explosion in order to gain enough height to allow the elbows to rotate into position (if that is the technique used) to begin the follow-through to lockout. Well, look again. Powerlifting great Rickey Dale Crain and others have pointed out that the pectorals come into major play first in the bench press—or should—followed by anterior deltoids and triceps.

Not only is there pectoral contraction and arm drive, but also a spreading of the lats and a shoulder thrust upward. The bar can be raised several inches with this spread and roll technique alone. Thick, strong lats are important in this style of benching, especially while the bar is being lowered into position and in the initial thrust.

Not all lifters do this lat flare or roll, as it is variously called. Some do it on purpose, some don't know to do it, and some do it and don't realize it. Many of the best do use this technique. Record breaker Rick Weill wrote about it in *PLUSA* in the late '80s, for one, describing the use of the back spread and shoulder girdle movement as a timed and sequential part of the lift requiring considerable practice. Chiropractor, lifter, and writer Keith Wassung has written about it in his column on the *Cyberpump* Internet site. Using the movements I call the Bench Shrug, the Shrug Dip, Spring Set Shrug and even the Lat Shrug can develop this spread and thrust. However, full range of motion rows and chins for the lats and other upper back muscles should not be neglected.

On the other hand . . .

THE RETRACTION SCHOOL

As pointed out to me by USAPL lifter Collin Rhodes, there are two distinct arches in bench pressing. Everybody has seen the extreme bow or bridge that many lifters achieve in his or her lower back as they lie lengthwise on the bench. Collin is an example of this style. This raises the high point on the chest where the bar touches when lowered, and provides even a decline effect to the lift for some persons.

The second or "**Lateral Arch**" is formed as the shoulder blades *are pinched together back against the bench throughout the lift*, which also raises the chest. According to Rhodes, one should assume the lateral arch, pinched position before the handoff and reset it after the handoff to make sure of maximum positioning. Otherwise, the lateral arch may flatten out during the eccentric part of the lift. Also, he attempts "to pull the bar apart" while lowering it, as if to stretch the bar out longer. The tension created is translated through the arms to the upper back and provides him with stored "extra energy" when he starts the bar back up.

This benching style uses no shoulder roll, except possibly toward the very finish of the lift. Rhodes states that he never uses the shoulder roll during the execution of the lift until he receives the finishing rack command. He warns *against* translating the movement of the Bench Shrug into the actual bench lift. He believes it is wrong to "shrug" the bar up during the completion of the press and that the shoulders should be kept in "the utmost rearward rotation possible throughout" the bench press movement.

OK. *How do we do that?* What shrug training is possible to maximize lateral arch effectiveness and to maintain that pinched-together rear position? I had worked on nothing but my *Texas* book after my last training articles were published in 1993. When that manuscript was finished, I switched to literary fiction, and sent back only power-lifting contest reports from Asia and journalistic pieces about the Byzantine internal politics of the International Powerlifting Federation. Frankly, I was burned out on train-ing questions.

At Collin's prodding questions, I hit the gym and began tinkering with shrug tech-niques to apply to this "new" trend in benching.

Rhodes and I traded emails throughout 2001 and he experimented in his training with the shrug variations we discussed to strengthen his lateral arch. He tried half a dozen or more movements but settled on the following:

> 1) <u>Narrow Grip Chinning Bar shrugs</u> with 50-75 pounds on a weight belt for three sets of six.
>
> 2) <u>Williams Shrugs</u> on a chest supported T-bar rowing machine with a three to four-count **hold** at the top of each rep. He uses five to six 45-lb plates on the plate holder for two sets of six reps. That's 225–270 pounds.
>
> 3) <u>Cable Crossover Shrugs</u> using crossover cables in the high setting, standing. Collin puts about 240 lbs on each side and leans back slightly, trying to emulate a position similar to that when lying on the bench. He rotates his scapulae back into the lateral arch position, *holds*, and

repeats this shrug-and-hold pattern for reps. Three sets of eight. There is no crossover motion on these, of course. The machine he uses is a double-pulley model, so the real poundage in use is somewhat less than stated.

4) Regular Standing DB shrugs with a slight forward lean. Two sets of eight with a pair of 140 pounders, *done one arm at a time.*

He also does Bench Shrugs, but more for stability than for raw strength, using about 500 lbs. for three sets of six. All the shrugs are done on his bench support-work day (Friday) except for the Bench Shrug, which is done on his regular bench day (Monday).

Collin, 34 as of this writing, widely known on Internet forums as "Pooh-Bear," *improved his bench by 20 kilograms (44 pounds) in one year* on shrug variations. That is excellent progress for a veteran lifter in a drug-tested organization. He placed second in the 242 lb. class at the 2001 USAPL National Bench Press Championships with a lift of 255 kilos (that's 562 lbs.) and made 584 at the IPF Bench Worlds in New Zealand, December, 2001, while placing third in the 275s. Collin just missed a 283 kg (624 lbs) 4th attempt going for the world record. By the time you read this, I bet he'll have made it.

Summing up, then, it would appear that the Bench Shrug would be of more use to "flare" or "roll" technique benchers, as it is similar to part of the actual lift. It may be used by lifters using the "lateral arch" as a strength and stability builder, but it should not be incorporated into that pressing style. Also, when I say "Don't bend the elbows" with these movements, I should add that really means don't pull or push with the arms. Locking the elbows completely may be uncomfortable or even dangerous to the joint.

CHINNING BAR SHRUGS

Frankly, I am astonished that Collin or anyone else can do a "shrug" *up* toward a chinning bar using scapular rotation with a weight belt loaded with as much as 75 pounds, especially considering the difficulty many heavier people have doing regular chins with no weight. This is not an easy movement to learn for most people and I recommend—nay, insist—that the reader start out light on the overhead lat pulldown machine. Lean slightly back and pull toward the collarbones without bending the arms.

I further suggest trying a "normal" grip spacing for openers and experimenting from there. I have long arms. A narrow grip makes the move difficult for me.

This is another example of a shrug movement that has not been taken to its full potential by weight trainers.

CABLE CROSSOVER MACHINE SHRUGS

The lifter stands in "crucifix" position between the uprights in the machine with the cables set in the high pulley position. Or, like Rhodes, he leans slightly to the rear, emulating the position taken on the bench during a competition lift when establishing a Lateral Arch, and shrugs the scapulae together without bending the arms. The contraction is held for three or four counts. The weights are then returned to the starting position under control rather than just more or less released. Three sets of eight is a good working scheme. Please read chapter two for more on this.

I believe this movement, coupled with *holds*, will prove to be a winner.

SHRUG HOLDS

Just what the word says and means. This can be applied in any contraction with any shrug variation. Hold the contraction for an extra count—four may be optimum—before releasing into the negative part of the movement. This next statement is as unscientific as it can be, but I suspect these holds reach deep-seated muscle fibers that may not be completely worked in "normal" full-range exercise motions.

THE BENCH SHRUG

Yes, I explained this exercise in chapter two, but I'll repeat myself here because I suspect a lot of readers will have jumped straight to this chapter first.

Take the position on the bench. Hand spacing should be the same as regularly used for benching, or perhaps a finger width or two closer together. Lower the bar with straight arms toward your chest by dropping the shoulders down toward the bench and crunching the shoulder blades (scapulae) together.

Force the bar upward by spreading the scapulae out to the sides like a lat spread while raising the shoulders off the bench.

Use pectoral contraction to roll the shoulders up and in toward the sternum. Keep the arms straight at all times during the movement. The bar will travel only three or four inches either way. Not only will your initial drive be improved by raising the bar this way, but control when lowering the bar to begin the bench press will increase.

Do not use a bench shirt with this exercise. You may find yourself having to readjust it after every rep. Also, there is no reason to do a big lower back arch or bridge with this movement. It would restrict the spread and contraction.

Always use spotters when doing the bench shrug. It's performed with straight arms and can easily move off line. Power racks work great when lifting alone. Just set the pins slightly below the point of bar travel (with scapulae fully retracted together back toward the bench), lock out, and begin. Start out with a weight that can be benched 8 to 10 reps until you have learned the movement and then add poundage over time.

Yes, you could do a **"lockout shrug"** by setting the pins a notch or so higher; that would mean starting the movement with the scapulae slightly spread.

It's common for a lifter to eventually handle several reps in the bench shrug with the same weight as his best single bench press, or even more. I suspect that lifters who approach competition record levels will find 90% of their best single max the limit, but this will vary. I am talking about doing these without a bench shirt and see no reason to use one. In fact a shirt may make the bar difficult to reposition at the start of each rep.

Dr. Ken Leistner reported good results similar to those I mentioned in his publication, *The Steel Tip*, February 1986, where he suggested adding two sets of bench shrugs at the end of a bench workout. I concur. Some of my Lon Morris College team in Texas (1983-85) experienced a gain of twenty pounds in the bench after one month.

This had two causes: added shoulder girdle strength and control coupled with learning to use the upward shrug and roll during the initial drive. However, if you do not use the "roll" and opt for the "lateral arch," *this movement will still greatly strengthen the shoulder girdle for whatever purpose.*

It's possible to do this move on incline or decline benches but it's trickier to control and more limited in range. Olympic lifters may want to try it on the incline as a support move for the clean and jerk.

Weightlifters have been using scapular rotation as an exercise with the bar locked out overhead since the early 1930s, according to the late Chester Teegarden. Lowering and raising the bar in this manner greatly strengthens the shoulder girdle, but I advise starting light and working up. I'd advise caution using a snatch grip overhead, but lifters have done it that way for decades and many still do.

Heavy loads with an extra wide grip can cause injury to the shoulder. I no longer recommend an unusually wide grip bench shrug variation unless working with moderate weights. Close grips are worth experimenting with, as is the Shrug Dip.

THE SHRUG DIP

These dips are the direct negative of the regular standing shrug. These should be done immediately following parallel bar dips or decline benches. The lifter assumes the position for dips but raises and lowers the body on straight arms by allowing the shoulders to rise toward the ears and then lifting the body, forcing the shoulders down using pectoral, latissimus, and serratus contractions. The use of a heavily loaded weight belt is a must if Shrug Dips are intended as an assistance exercise for the bench press. Bodybuilders can use these, too (or any of the variations). I mentioned elsewhere that former Mr. America Bob Gadja and his Chicago gang called these Monkey Dips. They are a favorite with the Iron Jungle club members who posed for some of the photos in this book.

Cable Crossover Shrug. *Collin Rhodes uses a layback position to simulate his benching position.*

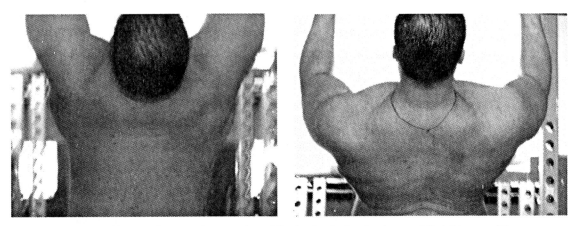

Chinning Shrug. *The two pictures show Rhodes in the beginning and finishing positions.*

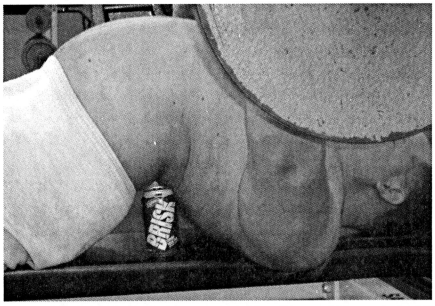

Horizontal Arch. *Rhodes trained for years to achieve this astonishing arch capability.*

Lateral Arch. *These shots demonstrate a bench position with no lateral arch (top) and then with full scapular pinch together (bottom), driving the shoulder girdle down into the bench by using the legs. (Bottom) is also the retracted position during the Bench Shrug.*

CHAPTER FOUR

SHRUG VARIATIONS FOR
OLYMPIC LIFTERS & POWERLIFTERS

Drawing of the Incline Shrug from 1981 course. Bench angles may be adjusted for different purposes.

SNATCH, CLEAN & JERK, AND DEADLIFT

I am not going to discuss the performance and technique of these lifts, as I assume most readers are familiar with them. These lifts are different but have similar stages. The first, for our purposes, is the initial drive off the floor to the point where the bar is roughly just below the knees. This varies depending on the size and proportions of the lifter.

The second phase includes thrusting the hips forward while driving the upper body toward the vertical.

Third, as the body extends vertically the shoulders are shrugged upward followed by arm pulling during the snatch and C & J. This usually happens too fast for the untrained eye to follow, but it is there. In the deadlift, the shrug part of the pull is directed to getting the shoulders back or erect, instead of up, and there is no arm pull.

At this point I'd like to ask three questions:

> **1.** Why do so many lifters practice only the standing shrug when the upper body in the first stage mentioned above is angled at 35 to 40 degrees in relationship to the floor and 55 to 65 in the second?

> **2.** Why do many Olympic lifters use only a clean-width grip in shrug training when the wide grip used in snatching causes a different direction of pull force during contraction of the muscles involved?

> **3.** Why are deadlifters not using their competition, over and under grip when shrugging in the gym? (Many are coming back to the hook grip; I approve, although lifters with short thumbs will have a problem.)

Do not misunderstand. I am not leading a crusade against the standing shrug. It's a specific movement within the clean and jerk or deadlift and is absolutely required in gym training so that maximum height may be obtained. However, as it works the upper trap primarily, *it may not be the best assistance movement for the lower stages of the lifts*. In the lower stages of the three lifts, the traps and lats are engaged in gaining and maintaining bar height as well as stabilizing the bar and keeping it close to the body.

Here's what I recommend in answer to the three questions above:

> **1.** Lie face down on a heavy-duty adjustable incline bench set at 35 to 45 degrees. A freestanding bench is best. This angle should match the angle of the spine in relation to the floor during the initial drive of the pull. Have your training partners hand up the bar.

> Mentally focus the contraction on a spot between the shoulder blades. Crunch the scapulae together. Don't contract up toward the ears. The lower the angle of the bench, the more the lats will be involved, especially if an underhand grip is used.

Don't forget: *practice finishing the movement with the shoulder blades forced down and to the rear.*

Get a full stretch every rep. Grip selection depends on which lift or muscle group is being targeted. Tony Garcy, the great USA Olympic lifting champion, used these moves in practice. He called them "retractors."

Next, move the bench up to 55 to 65 degrees for a set or two. This setting aids the second stage of the lifts as the lifter drives toward the vertical.

2. Because of the angle of the arms during the snatch, the direction of the shrug at the top of the lift is not just up, but also at an angle roughly from the hands to the base of the neck. The scapulae move toward each other as well as up. Olympic lifters should practice snatch grip shrugs at several angles as well as with the clean width grip. Wide grip is the way it's done during the snatch itself, so why not during the assistance exercise?

3. From what I read of top deadlifters' published routines, most do 25 to 30 lifts per workout. At least two-thirds of those lifts do not seriously challenge the lifter's ability to get his shoulders back. (Some powerlifting federations now require only that the lifter stand erect, and do not look for an exaggerated, shoulders back finish.) A few sets of lat pulls and shrugs are tacked on at the end. The standing shrugs are usually pulled up and then back. This not a good practice for powerlifters as it may develop the bad habit of causing the bar to drop at the completion of the lift and earn a red light. Rules vary on this between federations. (There is a trend in the last few years not to pull back to the rear when doing the standing shrug as an assistance exercise; I agree, especially if you are doing inclined or lean forward shrugs as well.)

Why not practice shrugs on a bench using the two angles above and work all the muscles of the upper back involved in drawing the shoulders to the rear? Lean-forward shrugs will increase all lifters' ability to "set" their shoulders at the beginning of the lifts and keep the upper back straight and the head up throughout.

These will improve your deadlift. My training diary shows a 55 lb gain in my DL after three months of practicing these movements at different angles the first time I tried them seriously.

You might practice the over-under competition deadlift grip regularly with the lean-forward shrugs for two reasons. One, obviously, is it's the grip used in competition. Secondly, there is a very subtle difference in muscle action between one side of the back as compared to the other when using the over-under grip. These shrugs will help keep the bar close to the body, which is very important. *However, more and more lifters find that the over-under grip causes a disparity in back development as well as uneven stress.* Some, such as 2000-01 IPF super-heavy weight champion Brad Gillingham of the USA, have switched to a double overhand, hook grip as used by Olympic lifters for this reason.

A Little Trick: This next has nothing to do with shrugs or traps but I'm going to shoehorn it in. Back in the days when the '55 Chevy was the hottest car in America and I was trying to switch my style from splitting to squatting with the snatch lift, old time holder of one -hand lift world records Roy Smith suggested I knurl my fingernails. Huh? That's right, take a nail or any sharp point and dig three or four grooves in your thumbnails the long way, from cuticle to the tip of the nail. When you clasp your forefinger over the nail for the hook grip, the grooves prevent slippage. If using the regular thumb-over-finger grip, groove your fingernails horizontally across the nail. Some lifters simply rough up their nails on the bar knurling back in the warm-up room.

We figured this trick was worth five additional pounds on a lift. Not much, you say? Many a world title has been won by that margin.

By the way, both powerlifting champions Chip McCain and Dan Austin have recommended lean-forward shrugs in articles in *Powerlifting USA*. I suggest using an incline bench or some other support so that greater weights may be used and more specific muscle groups targeted. Many lifters are capable of handling huge weights for sets and reps with shrug movements, so straps may be a good idea. Olympic lifting champion Alexyev of the old Soviet Union is known to have standing-shrugged 900 lbs for reps, as have other weightlifters.

Truly prodigious poundages are possible. There are no "world records" for shrugs, as no contest has ever been held for them as a *lift* that I know about, so we have only gym anecdotes. Rising powerlifter Josh Bryant reported as of January 2002 to have done 1035 lbs x 5 reps in the standing shrug and a *hold* off the rack with 1175! He was twenty years old at the time and weighed around 300 pounds.

I would be remiss if I did not point out that many top deadlifters do not regularly practice shrugs, preferring to practice pulls at different heights in the power rack. Some set their traps in a contracted upward position before starting the pull and try to hold that position throughout the rep, thereby getting a huge positive/negative benefit (see chapter two). Keith Wassung told me in an email in February 2000 that he does this during a partial deadlift from his knees!

THE HISE SHRUG—POWER STYLE

I said earlier I'd talk about shrug variations for the five competitive lifts. What kind of shrug variation could help the squat? I know of no shrug that can build hip and thigh strength.

But I do know one that will build confidence and upper body power and allow the lifter to manhandle a lot of weight. It's performed by shouldering a heavy bar and shrugging—or hunching—it upwards while taking deep breaths to build bulk and power. This movement will get new trainees past the stage of the bar hurting the shoulders, knit the shoulder girdle together and strengthen the entire upper torso.

Obviously I'm talking about the Hise Shrug (see chapter two). The story of Joseph Curtis Hise has been told many times, so I won't get into it, but he has been called the first powerlifter. The Hise shrug and high-rep breathing squats have been the key to many bulk and power courses since the 1930s. This was the first shrug other than the basic standing movement I ever attempted, way back in 1954. But for competition training, let's do it a little differently.

Unlike the breathing style Hise Shrug described in chapter two, back out of the rack with a weight you can squat for six to eight reps. Do not use a powerlifter stance; keep the bar in the normal position. Breathe in and shrug up toward the ears with trap and scapular action.

Eventually, many lifters will be able to handle weights in excess of the lifter's best squat. This will increase squatting ability as the lifter gains shoulder girdle stability, and his confidence will soar as he practices backing out ("walkouts") and setting up with overloads. Again, I do not recommend going so heavy that less than six reps can be performed. Six to eight reps should be sufficient; we are not trying for ribcage expansion here as described in chapters two and six.

The back shrugs I described will help keep the back straight and the head up during the squat. Combining them with the Hise movement helps prevent losing the bar forward over the head during the squat.

Wrapping it up, powerlifters might add two sets of Hise shrugs after the squat, bench shrugs or cable crossover shrugs when BP training and face down incline bench "Kelso" style shrugs and rack holds for deadlift assistance.

Olympic lifters will want to try snatch and clean grip shrugs at the positions discussed: initial, mid-point, and vertical. I say try them all, but get serious about those that meet immediate needs such as sticking points, getting the shoulders back, or the drive explosion in benching.

Well, that's about it for shrugs, although I mention them where appropriate in chapters five and six. Please use these shrug variations as an adjunct to your regular training. As a general rule, I would do them *after* the regular exercise they resemble most. I do not recommend trying very low reps or max attempts with these movements unless you are an advanced weight man, and then, be careful.

If you wish to do more reading about shrugs, Appendix II is a list of some of the articles I've written on the subjects in this book. The chapter "You Can't Shrug It Off" in my *Powerlifting Basics: Texas-Style* book from Iron Mind Enterprises, Inc, page 46, addresses training for the deadlift.

Articles about my work, or reprints, reviews and translations have also appeared in Dr. Ken Leistner's *The Steel Tip, The H. I. T. Newsletter, Iron Man, Powerlifting USA* (Doug Daniels 'work, among others) and in Japan in *Powerlifting News* and *Bodybuilding and Powerlifting*. I cannot confirm, but I have been told, that versions of my articles have surfaced in half a dozen countries and languages, including Chinese and Italian.

Articles plagiarizing my work and signed by other writers have appeared in several of the "better" publications in the game. I take it as a compliment!

Now I can get back to the gym and experiment more, and wait for the letters and emails telling me about the shrug variations I overlooked.

*Pat Henley at the top of a **Hise Shrug**, raising the bar with only shoulder girdle movement.*

CHAPTER FIVE

TRAINING WITH THE "TRAP BAR"
(OR SIMILAR BARS NOW AVAILABLE)

*(This chapter is based on the course I wrote for the Gerard Trap Bar, years ago when there were no other "trap bars" on the market. Yes, there are now a number of other such bars available, with distinct differences in design and possible advantages. However, the information in this course is applicable to all of them. **I use the phrase "trap bar" generically to describe all such bars as a class.**)*

At first glance, these oddly shaped bars that the lifter stands inside of may appear too small for a grown man to use. Actually, they have the potential to have a tremendous impact on the way we think about training. The theory is simple: moving the weights in closer to the body improves balance and less effort is necessary to move the weight.

While we are discussing biomechanics, let me add that by standing inside the bar frame, the weight is located to the rear of its normal path of movement. This reduces lower back stress and shearing forces on the spine and knees. Also, the improved leverage provides higher intensity muscle stimulation. In short, a person can train more effectively and with greater safety.

Time out here for a little background: In the mid 1980s, Al Gerard was a deadlift record holder in the ADFPA (drug free) in the southern states. He had lower back problems and had been searching for a way to train the deadlift without aggravating his condition. By developing the Gerard Trap Bar, engineer Al not only solved his physical problems but greatly increased his deadlift, as was his original intention.

I hate to waste space on this, but statements have been circulated in the iron world that Al's bar was originally designed as a trapezius bar only and not for deadlift movements. This is simply not true, nor is the implication that my 1993 "shrug system" book was only about shrugs. That, and the claim that others "later" discovered that the bar was useful for deadlifts and overhead presses is ridiculous, as nineteen pages of that shrug book were devoted to "trap bar" training, including those two movements.

In fact, Gerard's first ad for his bar, appearing in the September 1986 *Powerlifting USA*, advocated the deadlift, stiff leg deadlift, shrug, and "upright row." Dr. Ken Leistner and myself pushed for deadlifts, the overhead press, and high-pulls with Gerard's bar in magazine articles in 1988-89, well before any other parallel grip bars came on the market. Also, many of Al's early promotional materials emphasized the deadlift training aspect.

How do I know? I wrote them.

Unfortunately, there has always been a lot of defalcation of ideas and claim jumping among publishers and manufacturers in the iron world. Such nonsense only confuses the new trainees.

The Gerard bar was not in production as of August 2001, due to licensing and trademark disputes. It will be back, if it isn't already. I have never manufactured "trap bars" or any other equipment and I will not recommend one version or another here. There are many from which to choose, and the trainee should make a choice based on his needs and good sense.

But I digress. Let's get back to what these types of bars can do for the trainee.

Studies conducted by Gerard and others suggest the reduction in stress to the lower back varies from 14-18%. I assume this would depend on the proportions and leverages of the lifter plus the characteristics, balance, and shape of the bar used. Knee-shearing forces are reduced as well. In addition to doing leg, hip, and lower back work with the bar, Al discovered that the bar could be applied to other exercises. He has used all the "trap bar" movements described here in his own training.

The first thing I did when I got my bar was load up for the bent over or Lat Shrug for the middle and lower trapezius area and lats.

The response of the targeted muscle groups was just terrific! The palms facing feature of the bar provides the desired angle for maximum stretch and contraction while the braced bar delivers stability.

Some think that machines provide the stability needed. Perhaps. But my problem with machines has always been that a machine trains the muscle targeted or even the whole body to do what the machine does, and not necessarily what I would like it to do. This is the chief rap against the "Smith" machine, although some are better designed than others; I'd add that the trainee should also be careful of badly designed leg extension machines, some hack-squat machines (I can't *walk past* a hack machine without my knees hurting) and many pec-decs.

Regular standing trap bar shrugs can be done straight up toward the ears without dragging the bar up the body. With the iron closer to the body and moving vertically parallel to the spine without body drag, a more effective contraction can be achieved with less lower back stress. In the bent over position, the focal spot of contraction can be varied: to the lower trap inserts, the lats, the middle, or upper areas.

The *best* way to perform any bent over shrug variation is face-down on a high rowing bench or on an incline bench set a low angle. This takes the lower back and legs out of the exercise and isolates the muscles targeted.

I had known for some time that one of the most effective ways to shrug, at any angle, was with heavy dumbbells held with palms facing. But there are several problems with dumbbells:

1. It is sometimes difficult to get the bells into position without a spotter, as many experienced iron men can handle enormous poundages.

2. A lot of effort is bled off into the lats and other torso muscles as the trainee tries to stabilize the weights and keep them "in the groove."

3. Few gyms stock dumbbells over 100 lbs.

Yep, that's what I said. Many top powerlifters can rep shrug more than they can deadlift. And top Olympic lifters can often shrug more than they can clean. They better be able to, or they won't get very far!!

I know many experienced weight coaches hold that dumbbells are more effective than a straight bar for shrugging, but if one hundred pounders are all that's available, then there's a problem. Most advanced bodybuilders need more weight than that for optimal development. Lifters need way more. So how can a trainee, on any level of advancement, handle max poundages with stability and still get maximum intensity?

With a "trap bar," that's how. This bar is a real winner for home gym training, especially with the deadlift up on blocks for heavy hip and thigh work as spotters and squat racks are not needed. The original bar could be loaded to 700 pounds, which is enough for anybody to get a workout. (This poundage now varies, depending on the differences in competing bars on the market.)

Shrugs aside, *out of all the exercises a lifter can do with these bars*, I believe the finest is the deadlift, or leg lift. Because the trainee must get low to begin, and because the center of gravity is low, the result is a reduction in back stress. Further, a tremendous hip and thigh workout is accomplished safely and without the need of spotters. The leg lift on blocks puts more work on the thighs and is a fine substitute for squats and leg presses.

The "trap bar" is not only terrific for bent over shrugs but for overhead presses as well. This was the second movement I attempted with the bar other than those listed by Gerard. The shape of the bar allows it to be lowered to a point below that possible when performing behind the neck presses, and the hands to a point below and to the side of that possible when front or military pressing. One gets the benefit of heavy dumbbell pressing with palms facing each other but with much greater stability.

After three sets of eight reps with the bar the outer heads of my deltoids were screaming. Just when I was feeling smug about my "discovery," I received a copy of Dr. Ken Leistner's *The Steel Tip* containing an article recommending the overhead press with the Gerard bar. The good Doctor was way ahead of me, as he usually is. Differences in body proportions can make some devices less effective for some trainees. Very large or extremely heavy-shouldered people may find the hand spacing too close together for overhead pressing. (Some manufacturers now make a larger bar, and several companies make bars to order.)

"It's too small!" That is a common reaction for many when first seeing the Gerard bar. But for the exercises it was originally designed for, it will accommodate huge men. The bar became very popular in football weight rooms and has been used by players from pro teams like the Bears, Bengals, Broncos, Chiefs, and Dolphins. There are some monsters on those teams. Some powerlifting federations and schools have staged contests using these types of bars in deadlift competitions.

The Gerard bar and other such bars are a plus for football training because of the number of knee injuries and the wide spread bias against squatting among football coaches. As the bar greatly reduces shearing forces on the knees and lower back stress as well, it provides heavy hip and thigh work with improved safety.

Another feature of these bars is that no spotters are needed, and the bar is adaptable, if need be, to a number of stands and racks in the gym.

What I was trying to accomplish at age 54 —I put *The Kelso Shrug System* together in 1991—was to get back into good enough shape to compete again. As I only had time to train twice a week, I wanted to develop both size and strength without having to do a workout so grueling that it would take me a week to recover. I put together a program that largely succeeded in producing the sought-after results. (I did not compete again; a gall stone as big as my thumb, a new marriage, and a blown up appendix sidetracked me. I did gain ten pounds of muscular bodyweight and lost the same in blubber over a three-year period—in my mid-fifties! For more discussion of programs I used then, see my *Powerlifting Basics: Texas-Style* from Iron Mind, Inc. or Appendix One of this book.)

I've said it before, but choosing a program depends on what the lifter is trying to accomplish. As I have rotator cuff problems in both shoulders, the programs were designed to strengthen those areas affected.

I also had an inner ear operation in 1982 that made squatting and overhead work a risky business for several years due to faulty balance. Thus, the "trap bar" came along at the right time for me.

First, I'll list the programs I did at that time (1990-92) and then segue into heavy-duty schedules for powerlifting.

Monday

- Squats: 8, 6, 4, 12
- Trap bar stiff leg deadlifts: 2 x 8
- Bench Press: 3 x 6, 10
- Trap bar upright rows (high-pull): 3 x 8
- Deltoid cable pulls: 2x10
- Medium-wide grip pulldowns to front: 3x10
- Trap bar bent over shrugs: 2x8
- Incline DB curls: 3x8
- Triceps press downs: 3 x 8
- Standing Calves: 3 to 4 x 15-20
- Waist work: 3 to 4 x 15-20

I can already hear the snickers. This guy Kelso was trying to do a complete body workout every session. Only 30 or so sets! Well, friend, if you think this type of training won't work, wait till you see what I did on Thursday.

Thursday

- Trap bar deadlifts: 2 x 8
- Trap bar deadlifts on three inch block: 8, 2 x 6
- Incline Bench press: 8, 2 x 6
- One hand cable crossover (pecs): 2 x 10
- Trap bar overhead presses: 3 x 6 – 8
- One hand dumbbell rows: 3 x 8-10
- Trap bar standing shrugs: 2 x 8
- Barbell curls: 3 x 8
- Close grip bench press: 2 x 8
- Various calf work: 3-4 x 15-20
- Waist work: 3-4 x 15-20

To save time and energy, I often did biceps and waist work at home on a day off.

After a few months on this program, I gradually shifted to a more specific power-lifting routine and then into a full power cycle. The above program worked for me as I gained five pounds in the first two months I followed it and lost an inch off my gut. My knees quit hurting and I added forty pounds to my deadlift.

Now let's talk about training for competition powerlifting using Al Gerard's system. Here's how I would set it up:

Pre-Cycle Phase
(Train two days a week)

Day One

- Heavy squats:
- Trap bar stiff leg deadlift
- Bench press (speed work)
- Trap bar upright rows (high-pull)
- Assistance exercises: 2 sets each of close grip bench and calf work.

Day Two

- Trap bar deadlift (leg lift)
- Bench press (heavy):
- Trap bar standing shrugs
- Heavy rowing or pulldowns
- Assistance exercises: 2 sets each of military press and calves.

The total number of sets in these workouts should be twenty or less.

After three weeks, perform the stiff leg and deadlift movements while standing on a block or small platform at least three inches in height. This insures greater range of movement in both exercises and much more thigh involvement in the leglift. At this time I would drop the upright rowing and replace it with Lat Shrugs on an incline bench set at 35-45 degrees. I would also add a set of Bench Shrugs at the end of the bench press workout. (See chapters two and three for the Bench Shrug.)

Al Gerard stayed with his trap bar training for about three or four more weeks and then converted to a full cycle of about eight weeks to peak out at the contest he'd been shooting at all along. Lifters who think they need more squat training might want to set up a three or four day program.

Some lifters cycle up to a contest with regular deadlifts, and then switch back to the trap bar for the last two deadlift workouts before the meet. This reduces lower back stress while maintaining hip and thigh power.

Remember, the deadlift can be trained with the trap bar as much as twice a week due to the reduced lower back stress. Now, what about poundage selection? Here's what Al Gerard recommended ten or more years ago and I don't see much of a way to improve on it now:

Off-Season Phase

- Trap Bar stiff legs: 4 x 8 with 20-40% of your maximum single deadlift. Off blocks after 2-3 weeks.
  - Trap Bar upright rows: 4 x 8 with 20-30% of deadlift max.
  - Trap Bar deadlifts: 4 x 6 with 30-50% of deadlift max. Off blocks after 2-3 weeks.
  - Trap Bar standing shrugs: 4 x 12 with 30-40% of deadlift max.

(Start about 12 weeks before competition)

- Trap bar Stifflegs: 4 x 8, top set 50% of deadlift max (blocks).
- Trap Bar upright rows: 4 x 8, top set 35% of deadlift max.
- Trap Bar deadlifts: 4 x 6, top set 60% of deadlift max.
- Trap Bar standing shrugs: 4 x 12, top set 50% of deadlift max.

Peaking Cycle

The final eight weeks of the cycle is left up to the individual lifter to use a program he has found to be most successful in the past. Now get this! I will drop standing shrugs from the routine at this time and use only "Kelso" or Lat shrugs on an incline bench set at various angles. These are performed as an assistance exercise on the squat/bench day before my deadlift day.

The standing shrug is excellent for the upper trap, for Olympic style lifters, and for maintaining bar height. But the key function of the trapezius and other scapular retractors in the deadlift is getting and keeping the traps and shoulders squared or back, *not up*! That is why I practice several sets face-down on an incline bench set at 35 degrees and then several sets with it set at 55 degrees. These correspond to my body position during the initial pull and secondary pull of the lift as the body drives to the vertical.

There is no reason why bodybuilders cannot benefit from using the trap bar, even if it was originally designed for powerlifting. Deadlifts on blocks, stifflegs, upright rows, shrugs and overhead presses are all standard movements. The change in leverage provides advantages not found with straight bars.

Now I will go on to explain the trap bar movements one at a time:

DEADLIFT OR LEGLIFT

Perform as you would a deadlift with the straight bar. Your ankles should line up just behind the yokes that hold the plates. As your leverages are different with the trap bar, your form will allow your legs and hips to do most of the work. Start in the low position, back straight, arms straight, and drive with your legs as if you are trying to push your feet through the floor.

SHRUGS

Start as if deadlifting. After standing erect, shrug your shoulders up toward your ears. Keep your arms straight! Do not roll back during powerlifting training. (Some makes of bars now have extension attachments so the bar can be used in a rack.)

UPRIGHT ROW (HIGH-PULL)

Like the shrug movement, except bend your arms and lift the elbows high as you pull up toward your ears. Looks like you are doing dips with the trap bar in your hands or perhaps negative dips. Keep the elbows slightly to the rear, as in dips.

DEADLIFTS ON BLOCKS

Perform as you would the deadlift, except now you are standing on two to three inch plates or blocks. Even more hip and quad force will be used because of the extended range of movement. Keep the back as straight as possible, arms straight, and again simulate pushing your feet through the floor.

STIFF LEG DEADLIFT

Stand inside the bar with your knees slightly bent (unlocked), bend over at the waist, round your back, and then straighten up with control to a vertical stance.

STIFF LEG DEADLIFT ON BLOCKS

Same as above, except by standing on blocks you extend the range of movement and make the exercise more intense.

OVERHEAD PRESS

It is a little awkward to get the bar into position since it's not built for cleaning. You can place the bar on freestanding squat racks or perhaps inside a power rack. (Some companies offer extensions that adapt the bar for the power rack.) One way is to sit on the end of a bench with bar on the floor. Stand the bar up on the point of the bent crook of the bar nearest you. Grab the handles. Lean forward and put your head and shoulders into the bar so that the top crook hooks behind your neck across the shoulders. Then, push up and back with your hands and sit up erect, sort off a seated good morning. If you can't get the bar into position this way, you are using a heck of a lot of weight, or else you need stiff leg deadlifts and other erector work.

Ok, you have your head and shoulders inside the bar and are grasping the handles with palms facing, either standing or sitting. Allow the bar to sag down as far as possible, so that the handles are even with or just below the top of the deltoids. I grab the handles just forward of center so that the bar tips slightly to the rear. This enables me to press straight up with very little lean back. Return to the sag position after every rep. The outer deltoid will be strongly affected, with lesser benefits for the traps, triceps, and upper chest. Sets of 6 to 8 reps seem best. Again, very large or heavy-shouldered men may not be able to do this exercise with some of the smaller bars available.

BENT OVER OR LAT SHRUGS

Take the position for the bent over row or lie face-down on an incline bench set at 35 to 55 degrees. Select a weight that can be handled in rowing for eight reps. Keeping the arms straight, pull or shrug with the back muscles only and force the scapulae (shoulder blades) together. Concentrate on a point directly between the scapulae, focusing on the middle or lower traps. Lower the bar for a full stretch and repeat. See more on this in chapters one, two, and four.

Some may find it difficult to set up for this exercise, depending on their height or the benches available. Smaller men might stand inside the bar, taller men in back. If no comfortable way can be found, a straight bar or dumbbells can be used. Some companies make a cutaway bar for this purpose.

BENCH SHRUG

This move is described in chapters two and three. You may wish to use it after your bench presses.

A few comments are in order as I begin to wrap this up. Yes, you can use dumbbells for Bench Shrugs. You can use the trap bar if you can get it into position. Again, some models have extensions for use in a power rack. You cannot bench press with any trap bar as far as I know, except possibly with a cutaway model. I suppose an extremely tall or short person might be able to bench with it, or some of the new models, but 99 out of 100 people are going to risk smashing themselves between the eyes with the bend in the bent section of the bar. It depends on the person and the bar being used.

Unique Qualities of the Trap Bar

• It is designed as a deadlift training bar that provides reduced lower back stress and knee shearing forces. When practiced with the "pushing your feet through the floor" technique, it could be very useful to Olympic lifters for increasing their drive off the floor. This would also be of aid in training the squat, when using the deadlift movement on blocks.

• It may be used in place of equipment or in addition to equipment already in use.

• Because of the bar's balance, it provides leverage advantages that result in increased intensity—something everyone wants.

• The bar is safer to use for certain high poundage movements; this is especially true in home gyms.

Finally, I believe the bar has become a standard piece of equipment in the Iron Game, and will bring back lost enthusiasm for a lot of people who, like myself, were getting a little discouraged because of lingering physical problems. Besides, it is fun to use. I expect to see more deadlift records broken as word gets out about the trap bar.

Proper Form When Using A Trap Bar

1. Stand inside the bar with feet about shoulder width apart.

2. Your ankles should line up just behind the yokes that hold the weights.

3. Your grip should be in the center of the handles. If not the bar will tip.

4. Use lighter weights until you are familiar with the feel of the trap bar.

5. Use good form at all times. It becomes second nature as you go along.

More general basic courses using the "trap bar" are listed in Appendix I.

Deadlift or Leglift with Trap Bar. *Model — Al Gerard, inventor of the bar that carries his name.*

Deadlift on block. *Places more emphasis on quads and lower back.*

Hiroyuki Shinozaki demonstrates the overhead press with parallel grip bar. Excellent for deltoids. Hiro has placed second at 275 lbs. in the Japan Nationals.

Standing shrug with parallel grip bar. There is no body drag as with a straight bar.

Highpull works deltoids, traps, arms, etc. Good bulk movement.

CHAPTER SIX

RIB CAGE EXPANSION AND
OVERALL GROWTH

The vast majority of folks training with weights will never enter a lifting or body-building competition. They train to enhance their ability in other sports or for their health. Some train for t-shirt muscles and appearance and others to stave off the effects of time. Many want to improve their ability to do grip tricks to impress friends and win barroom bets, or to compete in strongman events, Highland Games, stone tossing or whatever. An immense unsung number of trainees are of the "garage" variety who enjoy getting together with pals and train only for their own satisfaction. Quite a few approach the "iron game" as a hobby and attempt a lot of exercises and out of vogue lifts from the "old days," collect antique weights and ancient courses, and are fascinated with the history of the game.

What follows is a presentation of an older training principle that many say is now outdated and which is out of favor in some quarters. On the other hand, it still has a large number of adherents, myself included, and has made something of a comeback in recent years. In my experience it is both result producing and an exhilarating way to train.

The following principles are designed to make your chest wider and deeper and spread your shoulders. It's a great program for beginners and first year men to use in stimulating overall growth and building a basic foundation for the future. Getting wider across and thicker front to back by expanding the rib cage will allow for more muscular weight to be carried. The exercises are for the most part not secret or new, although some of them have been neglected. They are arranged here in an order that will give maximum results.

In 1981, I copyrighted the "Bone Structure and Growth Course" in shorter form than this chapter. That title may be misleading, so I have dropped it here.

In truth, not much can be done with the bones, except maybe to make them stronger and to prevent osteoporosis as one ages. Very young trainees might achieve some lengthening. **The purpose of this method is not to change the bones, rather, it is to spur changes in the costal cartilages and others that attach the ribs to the sternum and spine, and in the small muscles that support the rib cage and in the inspiratory muscles that function during breathing.**

Expansion of the rib cage and will accomplish several things for you. Your appearance and posture will improve. A larger frame allows for more muscular weight to be gained. I want to emphasize that overall growth is a real bonus with these methods. Your strength leverage should improve. Your overall conditioning and endurance *will* improve. A by-product for bench press fanatics is that a larger rib cage and higher sternum will shorten the lifter's stroke. See chapter three for ideas on that.

For the routine to work best, the exercises should be performed as I explain them. Follow the instructions for three months (minimum) to six months. Results vary from person to person, but from my own experience and that of my pupils, I would say that one and a half to three inches of chest gain can be expected in that first time period. Reports in the literature from writers like John McCallum and John McKean claim more.

Critics of these methods often state that they can only be effective for trainees *under twenty three* or so years old, because the bones harden or set after that age. A number of recent articles state that older men cannot make any changes in their "bone structure," and suggest any noticeable improvements with these methods are just muscular weight gain. Yet the literature of training contains many stories of older men who claim success or at least satisfaction with this type of training. So, how can these differences in opinion be resolved?

Easy. *It's not about bones*, except perhaps in the young. In an exchange of emails, Casey Butt, a graduate student in electrical engineering from Newfoundland, reminded me that J.C. Hise wrote fifty or more years ago that the goal of rib expansion exercises is to place enough stretch on the costal cartilages to activate dormant mesenchymal cells that exist in the adult hyaline cartilage so that they differentiate into adult cells. Casey, who has written for *MILO* and has just started a new iron mag and web site, *The WeighTrainer*, adds that these and the inspiratory muscles that expand the rib cage during inhalation will—after some training—*aid in elevating and spreading the rib cage, lifting the sternum, and increasing lung capacity.*

I do not claim any scientific expertise, but if Hise was correct, that explanation will do me until a better one comes along. Scientists are generally wary of gym wisdom, but let me add an anecdotal story of my own. I was a concert folksinger for many years. Many times when I was out of shape, or had fallen back into the clutches of tobacco, I'd get a call to perform in a few weeks. I would hike out in the woods and bellow the score to musicals like "Oklahoma" or "Carousel" one day and head to the gym the next to do set after set of high-rep squats, pullovers, and Rader chest pulls. Worked like a charm for my breathing in performance and made me feel great. I assume my diaphragm was strengthened. My shirts became tighter *without* weight gain.

That suggests to me a reason why many older trainees claim rib cage improvement with these methods. If an older person has never trained before, activating the costal cartilages and supporting muscles of the rib cage should produce noticeable results. For a trainee who has had a very long layoff, regaining at least the structure possessed in the past should be an obtainable goal. Atrophied muscle can be pumped back up when training is resumed; maybe ribcages have "memories" as muscles do.

While preparing this chapter I corresponded with a gent who does not want his name used. His remarks were like many of the nay-sayers on this subject. He pretty much scoffed at the idea of costal cartilage stretching or growth and even the existence of "inspiratory muscles" which he claimed would be involuntary muscles in any case.

Then why, as I sit here at my desk pounding away at the keyboard, can I expand my chest measurement and lift my sternum voluntarily *without inhaling*? If a muscle or body part can be triggered voluntarily, then some way can be figured out to train it. (I think I just wrote a new "Kelso's Law.")

I got flack for my suggestion in the original "bone" course that a beginner might want to use a board under his heels while squatting. The complaint is that doing this may put excess strain on the knees and set the lifter up for injury. In fact, that thinking has become almost carved in stone in the last ten years, and is rarely contradicted. These things come and go in weight training. For instance, the box squat was a very popular training exercise when I was young. Then it was darned near illegal in gyms for decades because the "new" common knowledge held that they would injure the spine. But the box squat has come back in the last five years or so and is again widely practiced by powerlifters.

Now think about this: It depends how you squat. If you squat completely straight up and down—allowing your knees to get far ahead out over your toes—then you are transferring stress to your knees. If you break at the hips first and sit back into the squat, there should be little problem. I used both the elevated heel and the box squat for many years and have never had knee or back problems.

I have been in gyms where the instructors will not permit use of a board or plate under the heels, but regularly encourage use of the "sissy squat" or the Hack squat machine. Hacks kill my knees, no matter what stance I take. Again, a lot depends on the leverages of the trainee and the machine being used; this is another example where personal choice and need should make the decision.

Of course you have to learn to squat properly. I've been to two hundred-plus weightlifting and powerlifting contests and have yet to see a lifter walk out on to the platform carrying a two-by-four. But while learning to squat and developing flexibility along with the torso and shoulder girdle strength to support larger weights, a board, a small plate under each heel, or even strong-heeled shoes can help maintain balance and an upright position. But this won't work for everybody, since everyone has different leverages.

Many weightlifters and powerlifters still insert a heel lift into their shoes, which they say *helps them squat lower* and positions them to start driving their hips forward earlier during the ascent. A widely circulated story is that Dr. Squat, Fred Hatfield, regularly puts two-inch lifts in his shoes and was wearing them when he performed his famous 1,014-pound squat. I competed in weightlifting in U.S. Army combat boots. They worked for me then: if competing now, I'd choose a lighter weight shoe. Others insist that no heel is best and squat in no-heel basketball shoes, which in my case would throw most of the stress into my hips and lower back and cause forward lean. A powerlifer using a very wide stance probably would not benefit much from a high heel.

One overlooked factor: if your shoe size is small in relation to your height and overall proportions, the more likely you will benefit from a heel and stable shoe sole.

Brooks Kubik, widely respected author of *Dinosaur Training*, came out against raised heels in squatting in a *Hardgainer* article about ten years ago. He has since changed his mind, as this April 2002 quote reveals:

> *The stuff about squatting on raised heels being dangerous is tossed out by people who do not know how to do a proper squat. The exercise is perfectly safe. It's a lot safer (and more productive) to do a heels raised OL squat than to do the flat-footed "parallel" gut-it-up abominations that most guys do.*

Brooks is speaking here about the "Olympic"-style, high-bar, erect body, sink-it-to-the-calves squat as being preferable to the powerlifter's competition style for most trainees most of the time. Training for a powerlifting meet is another matter.

Heel height is an individual thing, although a ¾ inch heel is widely accepted as best and is the most common on the competitive platform. Several manufacturers make shoes specifically for weightlifting and powerlifting. The rules of the International Powerlifting Federation state that no part of the underside of the shoe may be higher than five centimeters. Two inches is 5.08 cm, so the IPF does not seem worried about lifters' knees. To end this, I'd say discard the board as soon as possible and get some good shoes with a firm heel that suits you.

As I have written many times, extremely wide hand spacing with any pressing or pulling movement, especially overhead or with the bench press, may result in shoulder injuries over the years. I believe that is especially true with long-armed individuals, or persons with a relatively long upper arm. Be careful, or find substitutes. In fact (and I am a long lanky type genetically) I did not put on major upper body mass until I included a lot of closer-than-normal hand spacing in my pressing and pulling movements. That's one reason I like the trap bar: the weights are in closer to the body. See chapter five for an explanation of the advantages.

Paul Kelso, left, age 15 1/2 (the young idiot obviously bitten by the bodybuilding bug), and his brother Mark, age 18. Note the narrow, flat ribcage structure on both boys. Paul's training log said he weighted 147 in this shot.

The author at 18 years 3 months, at about 192 lbs. The widened chest and raised sternum are plainly visible. See text for his program.

My first workout took place in the back yard of a pro wrestler named Joe Cassius, who lived near the SMU campus in Dallas. (Joe later became a famous psychologist and appeared on national TV talk shows.) He showed me how to row, squat, do pullovers, flies, dumbbell bench presses, and behind the neck presses.

I've got to throw this one in. Joe was very short (5' 4") and prodigiously muscular. Weighed about 215. A friend once suggested that if he ever needed work he could paint himself red, white and blue and get a job as a mailbox.

I mail ordered a barbell and set up in my garage. I had no squat rack or flat bench. My squat weight was limited to whatever I could clean and jerk and shoulder. I made up for this by doing as many squat reps as possible before dumping the bar off backwards onto the lawn. This set my father off swearing when the lawn mower wheels got caught in the holes and he threatened to use the plates for bass boat anchors. I had to mow the yard for years, but the high-rep squats were worth it. I could not have been doing any better exercise for a lanky, narrow-chested kid.

I "incorrectly" used a fairly wide grip for bent over rowing and behind the neck presses. My bench work was limited to pullovers, flies, and dumbbell bench presses on an old wooden Army ammunition box.

When I began training, I did not concentrate on t-shirt muscles, as so many beginners do, but on building the frame needed for overall development. I know things have changed a lot since the early fifties, but what good are "gladiator pecs" without structural strength and conditioning?

I had no workout partner to help with benching because weight training was frowned on in those days. High school coaches taught that weights would make you "muscle bound" (a term that has no medical basis) and would ruin your heart. How times have changed.

My improper training paid off. Without knowing it, I was using a training method that many men have used over the years. In five years I increased my chest size seven inches *before* regularly including the bench press in my program. Today my chest size is 48-50 inches, depending on my body weight.

"Breathing" squat programs for gaining bulk and power have been around a long time, the trail leading from Milo Steinborn in the 1920s to Roger Eell's course in 1932 to Mark Berry's writing in 1936, and then on to Peary Rader, Bob Hoffman and others. Joe Hise is famous for using them and behind neck presses to achieve huge weight gains.

This type of training is making a comeback. It usually features a single set of squats for twenty reps with forced breathing (see below). You can find more information on this type of training in Randall Strossen's book *Super Squats*, the writings of Peary Rader and John McCallum, and in *Hardgainer* magazine.

But I'm talking about ribcage expansion as well as weight gain here. With that in mind, let's get started. First, measure your chest, both normal and expanded. Use a metal tape if possible. Write it down. It's a good idea to keep a workout notebook or log to record your sets, reps, and poundages at the end of every workout. This is an easy way to keep track of your progress and makes interesting reading thirty years later.

Second, measure the distance from the base of your neck to the outside point of your deltoid (shoulder) muscle. You will be amazed at how much difference a gain of ¼ to ½ inch in width will make in your general appearance. Measure yourself again after three months and see what happened.

Third, eat! (Unless you are over weight in which case you should use a common sense diet without fads.) Chicken, fish, milk, eggs, cheese and canned, water-packed tuna are excellent sources for the protein and minerals you need for muscular gain. Eat vegetables every day whether you like them or not. Put fruit on your cereal. Eat a baked potato, pasta or brown rice three or four times a week for training energy. Drink a "blender bomb" made from milk and protein powder every day.

Stay off the soft drinks and bakery stuff for a while. They have too much sugar and too many empty calories. Do take a vitamin-mineral supplement.

Following is your suggested list of exercises. I'll explain them step-by-step:

1. Stretching and Trunk Twists.

2. Breathing Stiff-Leg Deadlift. 1-2 sets.

3. Breathing Squat. 2 sets. Alternate sets with:

4. Light pullovers or Dumbbell flies, or breathing-style Hise Shrugs, Rader Chest Pulls, etc.

5. Breathing Overhead Pulldowns behind neck wide grip, or on the cable crossover machine. 1-2 sets.

6. Alternate between A and B:

    A. Incline Bench Press and Bent Over Rowing wide grip. 2-3 sets.

    B. Behind Neck Press wide grip and Heavy Bent Arm Pullover with barbell or on Nautilus Torso machine. 2-3 sets.

    (Do 'A' one workout day and 'B' the other.)

7. Rader Chest Pulls (optional). 1 set.

8. Calves, Curls, and Waist. No more than 2 sets each.

Yes, you can increase the number of sets when you feel ready.

You're probably thinking that this a strange course because there are no bench presses, leg curls, or one-hand concentration curls. There is a sound reason for omitting these and other exercises. They don't fit the purposes of this course.

Neither does extending yourself on your work set(s) to the point of puking or maxing out regularly with low reps or singles. Instead of "no pain, no gain" I hold that "train, not strain" is the best axiom to follow with this program.

Beginners, first year men, and most other trainees should remember that courses published in the magazines are usually written *by* advanced men *for* advanced men. (Many, if not most, of the articles in the glossy magazines that are signed by "Mr. Wonderful" are actually ghost written.) I don't care if Arnold, Flex, and Ronnie recommend twenty sets per body part. They have been training hard for years and are conditioned for it. You probably haven't been.

This course is designed for people on the way up who want a good start. Specialization and training for other goals can come later.

Now for the method:

STRETCHING

Before beginning any workout session, warm up thoroughly. Do some free hand knee bends, toe touches, pushups, and wrestler-type stretches on the floor. Don't neglect the shoulders. I like to do some squat-style snatching movements with a light bar. Get loose first so you don't injure something later.

TRUNK TWISTING

Place an empty bar or broom stick across your shoulders. Twist in a deliberate fashion back and forth from the hips up. Pick a spot on the wall in front of you and keep your face and hips aimed at this spot. Don't bend your knees. Twist around far enough so that your hands cross in front of that spot on the wall. Leaning forward or back slightly will stretch or contract different areas of your waistline and torso. Begin with about twenty counts each way, eventually working up to fifty.

Do the same thing bent over from the waist. Your goal is to get loose enough so that the bar swings past the opposite toe. This works the love handle area. Try to contract your abdominal muscles on the down swing. Do the same number of reps as above.

Many bodybuilders and coaches are against this movement, claiming it thickens the waist and can lead to spinal injury. It can, if you use a lot of weight and swing the bar ballistically. I believe the entire waist column should be worked in order to better support heavy squats and overhead lifts. You can always cut back. After all, what are you training for, athletic power or the beach?

These exercises warm up your waist, hamstrings, and lower back, which leads to a great—but little practiced—breathing movement.

THE BREATHING STIFF LEG DEADLIFT

This exercise is well known for developing the lower back, hamstrings, and leg biceps. Our way will do the same, but it is also a heavy-breathing chest expander. If you've never done any toe-touching with weight before, start light. Use an empty 20 lb. bar, an Olympic bar, or more, depending on your strength. Try it first with a wide foot stance (which means you won't have to bend over so far). As you loosen up, move your feet closer together.

The first several workouts will stretch and contract your hamstrings and spinal erectors and you'll feel it the next morning. Bend your knees a little if you need to, but work toward keeping the legs almost straight. As you increase the weight over the weeks, I'd suggest keeping your knees unlocked but stable. This exercise also strengthens your hamstrings, glutes, and lower back; all are important in squatting.

The important part of this movement is timing your breathing with the motion. When the bar passes above your knees on the way up, breathe in. Keep your arms straight, roll your shoulders to the rear, and breathe out forcibly while contracting your lats and pecs and squeezing the sides of your chest with your arms. Your ribcage should be forced forward and upward at this point. The sternum or breastbone will be pushed out and up. Hold the pressure for a count or two. Then lower the bar and repeat.

This movement takes practice to master. It's all one smooth movement until you get to the exhale-and-contract point. To achieve maximum chest lift, *there should be no air in your lungs during the contraction.* For extra gains, inhale, exhale and flex again while in this position. Do this several times each rep. It's very important to use as much weight as possible so that the contraction and chest lift will be maximized. You can do this from a regular or conventional deadlift motion as well, using the legs and more weight. (You can do it without leg or lower back involvement—see the "**sternum shrug**" in chapter two—but some leg/hip use works best for the purposes of this course.) Try 12 reps per set.

Warming up the legs and lower back is necessary as it leads us to the monster move of the course:

THE BREATHING SQUAT

Most advanced men as well as trainees agree: They hate squats. There is nothing in the world so creative as a trainee inventing excuses for not doing squats. They pinch a nerve in my back. They aggravate my football injury, my old war wound, my car accident injury. Pick one, any excuse will do. One popular excuse is that they will make your butt big. And it's true that if you perform squats incorrectly for several years you can develop hips and thighs out of proportion to the middle and lower thigh.

However, doing powerlifter competition-style squats (bar held down the back with feet spread wide) isn't going to produce the thigh that 99 out of 100 mirror athletes want. Furthermore, most of you couldn't build a big butt if you wanted one. Your heredity, or natural structure and shape won't allow it. In fact, if you do have a flabby seat, high rep squats will help tighten it up! Did Steve Reeves, John Grimek, or Reg Park have big butts? Does squat champ Ed Coan have one? Does Sivokon? No.

The truth is, properly performed squats are the best single exercise known for overall growth and power. There is no getting around it. The key is doing them properly for the purpose you have in mind. Never, never attempt high-count, 15-20 rep heavy breathing squats in the style of a powerlifter's competition squat. Here is how to do them for the goals of this course:

Choose a weight that you can squat for 10-12 reps. The bar must be heavy enough so that the last 4 or 5 reps are serious. *Now, what you are going to do is 15 reps—by taking 3 or 4 extra breaths between the last 7-8 reps, and possibly a little help from your training partner.* If you have never trained at all, I suggest starting with about one-third of your bodyweight. Not a few trainees have started with an empty bar.

Take the bar off the rack, making sure it rests across the trapezius, not high on the neck, but not down the back like a powerlifter either. If you don't have a squat rack then either build one, learn to clean and jerk real quick or join a gym, but do something. If the bar hurts your spine or shoulder bones, try wrapping a thick towel around the bar. You'll soon get used to it, and the deadlift/shrug movement in the breathing stiff leg deadlift will soon thicken your traps. This is where you should start experimenting with heel heights.

Shoulder the bar and back away from the rack. Your heels should be directly under your armpits and not placed wider than your shoulders. The very tall or long-legged may have to go wider. Use fairly wide hand spacing on the bar. Take a deep breath. Lower yourself into the squat while keeping your back and upper body as straight as possible. Stay under control. Don't just fall down and bounce back up. Lower yourself until your thighs are at least parallel to the floor (a line from knee to hip joint) or just under, and then rise. (Half squats as often practiced and too often *taught* at commercial gyms won't get it.)

Breathe out on the way up. Back flat, body erect as you come up. Keep your head up. Keep your chest up. Do not breathe in or out in the bottom position.

A well-known trick in doing squats is to pick out a spot on the wall in front of you that is about forehead height. Stare at it while squatting. Keeping your head up helps you stay erect and your back straight. Do not throw your head back and look up at the ceiling.

Don't neglect your ab work, ever! The abdominals balance the pull of your lower back and if one or the other is weak, you can injure yourself. It's my opinion that training belts are over-used. Rather than supporting your lower back, their real function seems to me to be to give your abs something to push against.

It's a matter of choice. I never use a belt while squatting unless using a weight I can handle for six reps or *less*, or with heavy overhead work. The lesson is clear: work on your abs.

The important thing about these squats is the breathing. Breathe in at the top, squat, and breath out starting about halfway up. As you reach the sixth rep, take an extra breath and exhale before starting the next rep. After the tenth rep, take two or three extra breaths. By the fifteenth rep you may need five extra breaths. You must experiment until you find out how much extra weight to use to force this extra breathing and still do 15 reps.

Once you reach this level, add a little weight every other workout or so. I don't care if it's only 1 pound on each end. (Some add half-pound "washers" on each end and scooch the poundage up a hair at a time; this method has made a comeback of late, but was widely known back in the 1920s and '30s, especially in England.) Stay at 15 reps and slap on weight as often as possible. Do two sets of 15 reps. After each set of squats, go to a flat bench and do a set of straight-arm pullovers or dumbbell flies.

John McKean has suggested doing a set of pullovers *before* squatting as a sort of ribcage warmup. As I recall, he stated that doing this might act as a trigger for growth. If he is right, *then why not try a set of pullovers during warm-ups for benching for the same reason?*

Stick with this squat method for three months and your chest must expand and your overall condition improve.

STRAIGHT ARM PULLOVER AND FLIES

Lie down on the bench lengthwise—do not lie across it. You might put your feet up on the bench. We want to stretch the ribcage here, not the abdominals.

Hold a small weight (a ten to twenty pound plate or dumbbell should do) with both hands at arms' length over your chest. Keep your arms straight or slightly bent.

Lower the weight back over your head as far as it will go. Breathe in while lowering the weight. Stretch at the bottom. Then raise the weight while breathing out.

Repeat 12-15 times. I wait to breathe in until the weight passes over my face. This is not a muscle builder but an expansion exercise. A heavier weight turns this into a pec-lat movement.

The pullover tends to lift and deepen the rib cage. Dumbbell flies expand and widen the chest. Try them some workouts instead of pullovers. Lie on a flat bench while holding a pair of light dumbbells at arms' length. Keep your elbows slightly bent with palms facing each other. Lower the weights to each side while breathing in. Let the weight stretch your pecs and ribcage at the bottom of the movement. Exhale while raising the dumbbells back to the starting position. Repeat for 12-15 reps.

The legendary John Grimek used to do a decline fly including extending the bells well behind and below his head. (Upside-down negative laterals?) A photo in an old *Strength & Health* showed him doing these hanging head down from a chinning bar, his feet strapped into "iron shoes" attached to the bar. How he got into that position I don't know. Those "inversion shoes" or hooks that were popular on TV "infomercials" a while back would work for that.

Remember, a set of pullovers or flyes is to be performed after each set of squats.

RADER CHEST PULL

Peary Rader, founder of *Iron Man* magazine, developed the chest pull as another ribcage expander and sternum lifter. Simply grab on to any immovable object forehead height or slightly above. Pull down and in with both hands while exhaling. Your chest will rise up and out. I believe a palms-facing grip works best. Do sets of 12 reps.

EXTRA—THE HISE BREATHING SHRUG

See chapter two for the explanation of this movement. I would do it instead of one of the other breathing exercises like the Rader Chest Pull, or the Breathing Stiff Leg Deadlift. Two breathing movements per workout should be enough. In fact, doing both the Breathing SDL and the Hise Breathing Shrug in the same workout is likely too much. Again, 15 to 25 reps are best for a breathing program.

EXTRA—RACK RAISES

This is the exercise with which Casey Butt of Canada has been experimenting. I have never seen it mentioned elsewhere in the literature on this subject. He thought of naming the exercise after himself, but rejected that idea for obvious reasons. In this case, the "rack" referred to is the bones of the shoulder girdle and ribcage from which the muscles hang, not a metal power or squat rack.

The bar is held across the anterior deltoids as if setting up to do front squats. The lifter inhales and raises the bar upward with the shrugging motion as in the Hise Breathing Shrug. As the bar is not across the back, there is greater freedom of movement as the bar is over the rib cage and not pressing down on the spine. It is way too early to tell, but this expansion movement may prove superior to the old Hise style.

EXTRA—THE BENCH SHRUG

Include this in expansion training if you wish, using your bench press hand spacing, but keep the weights moderate and use high reps, 15-20. See chapter two for the how-to-do-it.

Heavy weights with a wide grip may injure your shoulders. I worked up to some large poundages this way once and heard a big "FPOP" as the upper arm bone separated from the socket or whatever the heck you call it in the shoulder joint. Popped back in to place on its own, but the shoulder was sore for a week.

BREATHING OVERHEAD PULLDOWNS

This is another "unknown" exercise. After your squats and pullovers or flies, walk around a little and get your breathing under control. You should be puffing pretty hard; if not, you ain't working hard enough!

Next, go the overhead lat machine. Find a weight you can use for 2 sets of 12. Beginners should try one-third of their bodyweight. Use a wide, but not ridiculously wide, palms-away grip that you can handle. Sit directly under the bar, low enough that the weight will not rest or bounce off the plate stack.

Inhale. That's right. Breathe in while pulling the bar down to the back of your neck or to your chest. Try to touch your trapezius or sternum. Then exhale and allow the bar to rise to arms' length and stretch you out at the top. Breath out while the bar is on its way up. (Yes, this is backwards of the normal breathing pattern.) Lean forward and s-t-r-e-t-c-h. This move will spread your shoulders wider while working the upper back and the lats.

This backwards breathing could be used with pullovers and flies as well. I recommend using the "normal" breathing pattern about half the time with the overhead pulldown; doing both styles adds to the eventual results.

If you train at home, you have a problem. You could do wide grip chins, if you can do them. Some substitute moves include wide grip bent over rows, one hand dumbbell rowing, two hand snatches, the snatch grip standing shrug, shrugs while hanging from a chinning bar, and so on.

<u>CROSS OVER CABLE PULLS AND SHRUGS</u>

I've found that doing pulldowns and shrugs "to the side" on a cable crossover machine is extremely good for getting wide and for carving out the smaller muscles of the upper back for bodybuilding purposes. Set the machine in the high position and stand or kneel in the middle. Pull the handles straight in while trying to touch the elbows together behind the back. Then, try it as a *shrugging motion* for a set, using straight arms to full stretch and then rotating and pinching the scapulae together without bending the elbows. A word of caution: start light!

<u>Note of warning:</u> Do not try to do all these movements in any one workout. Breathing Stiff Leg Deadlifts and Breathing Squats, plus pullovers or flies and one other movement of your choice are plenty. Excessive stretching can cause an extremely painful condition where the costal cartilages attach the ribs to the sternum or breastbone. Anyone who has laughed while having broken ribs will understand. Nothing but a long rest can cure it that I know of, and that will set back your training.

That this condition can occur from this type of training tells me that the cartilages are being stretched and that these methods work.

I have divided the next part of the course. One day do Incline Presses and Bent Over Rows. The second workout day do Behind the Neck Presses and heavy Bent Arm Pullovers. Alternate these two groups every other workout day.

Day One

Incline press and bent over row, 2-3 sets each of six to eight repetitions.

Day Two

Behind the neck press and bent arm pullovers, 2-3 sets of six to eight reps.

INCLINE PRESS

You may set the bench at a variety of angles to get different responses. Use a grip about one finger wider than your usual flat bench press. Inhale while lowering the bar to your upper chest. Exhale as you press up. Keep the bar above your nipples.

Start with about 70% of your flat bench exercise weight, not of your best single. Beginners should try about 33% of bodyweight.

This movement will work the upper and middle pecs and contribute to that slab-like tie-in with the front deltoid that improves your appearance so much. However, the vaunted "pec-delt tie-in" bodybuilders seek often depends on genetic structure.

BENT OVER ROWING

Pick up the barbell as if you are cleaning, but use a wider grip, about the same as you would with the bench press. Bend over from the waist, feet spread for balance. Start with about one third of your bodyweight until your lower back is used to the position. Bend your knees slightly. Pull the bar up to your belly button while keeping your elbows pointed out. Then lower the weight while breathing in and get a good stretch in the hang position.

Wide grip rowing will widen the shoulder structure and develop the rear deltoid, lower trapezius, and lats. Yes, wide grip shrugs for a set or two would be positive. Later on in your workouts, you will want to get more lat concentration by using a closer grip and angling your elbows in at about 45 degrees.

If you experience stress in the lower back with these, it may be that your lower back and hamstrings need work, or your leverages are not good for bent over rowing. I have short thighs and a long torso and that is not good for this movement, unless I keep the spine at a 45 degree or more angle above the floor and keep the bar very close to my legs. Using the wide grip on a seated rowing machine or other apparatus might be better.

BEHIND THE NECK PRESS

The behind the neck press is regarded by many as one of the two or three basic deltoid exercises. The entire shoulder girdle is involved: upper chest, the three deltoid heads, upper back, and triceps. Some will argue that there are better moves for the side and rear deltoid, but this movement will spread the entire area as well as develop muscle.

Grab the bar with moderate hand spacing just a little wider than your military press grip. (Again, do NOT use an excessively wide grip.) Start with about 35% of your bodyweight or a weight that is a tough eight reps. Clean or snatch the bar overhead or take it off the rack. These can be done seated.

Press the bar overhead to a full lockout. Breathe in while lowering the bar behind the neck. Look in the mirror and watch the bar to a point even with the bottom of your ears. Then explode the breath and push the bar up. Some lower the bar to the traps. This will bring the upper back into play more but I believe it stresses the shoulder joints.

Note of warning: There is a lot of concern in some quarters, and in my mind as well, that long-term use of movements with extremely wide hand spacing can lead to shoulder injury or rotator cuff problems. That is why I have omitted wide grip bench presses to the collarbone, which are popular with bodybuilders. I do not think that using the wide grip moves listed here for the purposes of this course will cause problems, *because it is not my intention that anyone use this course exclusively for years.*

BENT ARM PULLOVERS

This is an "old" exercise that is not seen a great deal these days. The use of pulley lat machines and offset torso machines has taken its place in most gyms. Nevertheless, the bent arm pullover develops lats, upper back, pecs, serratus magnus, and expands the rib cage.

Lie flat on a bench. Hang your head over the end. Hold the bar on your chest. An EZ curl bar works well. Start with 25% of your bodyweight or lighter until you get used to the movement. Then pile on plates as you go along. Take a grip with hands about 10-12 inches apart. Pass the bar over your head and down toward the floor. Keep your arms bent so the bar passes close to your face. Breathe in going down and out as you pull the bar back to the chest.

I, and others, have flopped face-up on the leg curl machine with our feet at the "wrong" end and used our arms to do bent arm pullovers. This John McCallum favorite works great but the problem is finding a machine that will let you get in position.

This movement is a great strength builder as well as body shaper. I understand that the unofficial world record is around 400 pounds (by former Olympian weightlifter Steve Stanko) and that was pulling the bar from the *floor* to the chest! If you belong to a gym with a pullover type torso machine, use it for several weeks before going to the Bent Arm Pullover.

This is important: Breathing Stiff Leg Deadlifts, Breathing Squats, Hise Shrugs, Rack Raises, and even Rader Chest Pulls are breathing exercises. Pullovers, flies, cable pulls to the side, etc., are stretching movements. Overhead "breathing" pulldowns do a little of both. I suggest that *two exercises from each group in one workout are plenty.* Be careful not to overtrain your rib cage. As I said above, excessive forced expansion movements can lead to over-stretching or even tearing the cartilages, causing a very painful condition only rest can cure.

All the exercises listed under Day One or Day Two should be performed for two to three sets, six to eight reps, unless otherwise indicated. You should be breathing hard after squats and pullovers and walking rubber-legged. You will be pretty much worn out after the presses and pulls—if you have been working hard enough.

Finish off your workout with one or two sets of moderate weight biceps curls and calf raises. Do some sit-ups or other waist exercises. What's next? Get out of the gym. Don't do much on your off days. Get plenty of food and sleep. You will grow.

How often should you train? There's a lot of argument in weight room circles about the correct number of days a week to train; almost as much difference of opinion as there is about sets and reps. If you are a beginner with less than three months training, or trying these methods for the first time, I suggest a three-day-a-week schedule as listed above. After you have been training awhile, or if you are experienced, you will eventually want to increase poundage and add sets. When you get to that point, you might cut back to five workouts in two weeks or even to twice a week, using as much weight as you can handle properly. You should realize quick gains.

Some find that a single set of straight-arm pullovers on off days is a big help. My high school pals and I would try a few Rader Chest Pulls wherever we were—at the pool on the high-dive ladder frame, the softball backstop, anything we could grab on to that gave us the correct angle.

What about after the three month or more trial period? Use a regular workout for a while. Try some powerlifting or Olympic-style weightlifting. But once or twice a year, come back to this course and high-rep squats. When you can do several sets of 15-20 rep bodyweight squats you will be well on your way to real health, strength, and a powerful appearance. Reach one and a half to double bodyweight on the bar and you should have moved up a couple of weight classes. Many men work up to a single set of 20 reps with 400 pounds as a goal and believe me, they are terrific specimens when they accomplish that.

At least twice a year I come back to the methods described in this course. They worked for me when I was a young man, and they still work for me.

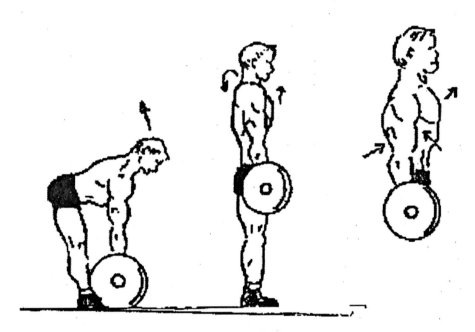

Breathing Stiff Leg Deadlift. Keep knees unlocked. Drawing from 1981 "Bone Structure" course.

KELSO'S SHRUG LAWS

A "shrug" is not an Italian mannerism or some kind of bird.

"Strength lies in the nape of the neck."—The wizard Merlin to the young King Arthur, in *The Once and Future King* by T. H. White.

The "Kelso Shrug" is not a single magic exercise but a principle of training with many applications.

Most trainees are not even approaching their potential in "shrug" movements.

Shrug "HOLDS" will be a standard training technique of the future.

When doing a major exercise, the smaller, assisting muscle groups may give out before the large groups you are trying to reach.

Add a set or two of these shrugs after any exercise they resemble most: Lat Shrugs after rows, Bench Shrugs after bench presses, etc.

You can focus on the area you wish to work through mental concentration and changing the angle of attack.

Don't jam your head forward while shrugging; keep your head and neck erect.

The standing shrug is a great all around movement; but it may not be the best for the beginning stages of the pull for deadlifts, cleans and snatches.

By setting the incline bench at different angles corresponding to stages within the pull, a lifter can attack sticking points in the vertical pull.

Contract the shoulder blades down and back when finishing a movement in bent over or lean forward positions or on the incline bench.

The beauty of these variations is that you can target a specific muscle or area and then zero in on it by adjusting your angle of attack and mentally concentrating the contraction right where you want it.

Experiment with the shrug principle on any equipment available in your gym: if a muscle or body part can be triggered voluntarily, then some way can be figured out to train it.

All shrug variations have not yet been discovered.

COURSES

*T*he *following are courses I have personally used for strength and growth. They tend to be abbreviated and are not for pre-contest training. They are not carved in stone and the reader is free to alter them for his own needs.*

A Strength and Growth Course Using the Shrugs and Other Exercises in this Book. Train 2-3 days a week.

Day One:
> 1) Breathing Stiff Leg Deadlift
> 2) Squat
> 3) Overhead Press (I like DBs)
> 4) Rowing
> 5) Lat or Bent Over Shrug (incline OK)

Day Two:
> 1) Bench Press
> 2) Bench Shrug
> 3) Deadlift or High-Pull or Power Cleans
> 4) Hise Shrug
> 5) Biceps Curls

Sets and reps your choice. Calf work once a week.
Waist work either day or at home.

***

General Training Using The Trap Bar.
This is a twice-a-week or five-times-in-two-weeks program.

Day One:
      1) Regular Squats, warmup + 3-4 sets of 6-8 reps
      2) Stiff Leg Deadlift with trap bar, 1-2 x 10-12
      3) Bench Press, warmup sets + 3 x 6-8
      4) Various rows and pulldowns, 3-4 x 8-10
      5) Trap Bar Press overhead, 2-3 x 8

Day Two:
      1) Trap Bar leg lift, warmup + 3-4 sets x 8-12
      2) Incline DB Press, same
      3) Trap Bar High Pulls (upright rows), 3 x 8
      4) Trap Bar Standing Shrug, 2 x 8-10
      5) Biceps Curls, 2-3 x 8

Those pursuing chest expansion might do squats two or more sets with 12-15 reps (or even 1 x 20) alternating sets with pullovers or Rader Chest Pulls, Hise Breathing Shrugs, etc. I do calf and ab work once a week at the gym and at home on off days.

An Abbreviated Course for Growth and Power.

Day One:
      1) Trap Bar Deadlift (leg lift)
      2) Bench Pressing of choice
      3) Rows or Pulldowns of choice

Day Two:
      1) Squat
      2) Parallel Bar Dips
      3) Trap Bar High-pull (upright row)

Usually done with 4 x 8 or 5 x 5 set-rep schemes. I often alternate dips and trap bar high-pulls as they are positive-negative to each other.

I trained two workouts a week or five times in two weeks, alternating days. I found more rest necessary as I got older. The reader may choose his own pace.

Kelso's Favorite Abbreviated Course

I used to travel a lot as a musician or fishing tackle salesman. This course worked great when I was pressed for time. It will work whenever. If pursued for several months, pushing up the poundage on the primary lift will work wonders.

Select a weight you can clean and then military press for ten reps. Take off about ten per cent. Clean the bar from the floor and then press. That's one rep. Repeat, from the floor. About the eigth rep you will probably need to begin push-pressing, kicking a little from the knees. Around the fourteenth rep begin jerking the bar overhead, split style. As the bar gets "heavier" around the eighth rep or so, you should probably be doing a full squat clean by that point and through to the end.

Try for twenty reps. The theory is like that of 20-rep squats; the last 5 reps should be *tough*. If you start with 100 lbs, it should feel like 200 on the last rep. It's OK to pause or rest between reps with the bar on the floor. Set up every rep and use good form. Add a little weight every workout or so. Finish your workout this way:

> Do a set of breathing flies—15 reps.
> Do two sets of abdominal work—15-25 reps. (A crunch and a leg raise.)
> Do one set of DB biceps curls for the sake of vanity. 10-12 reps.
> Get out of the gym. One rep.

See chapter five for more trap bar courses and chapter six for a program that is excellent for beginners and first year men.

Remember, any of the shrugs discussed in this book may be added for a set or two following the full range of motion exercise they resemble most.

APPENDIX II

"SHRUG BOOK" RELATED PUBLICATIONS
BY THE AUTHOR

BOOKS:

The Kelso Shrug System, Middle Coast Publishing, 1993. (Out of print.)

Powerlifting Basics: Texas-Style, Iron Mind Enterprises, Inc., 1996.

ARTICLES & COURSES (A PARTIAL LIST RELEVANT TO THIS BOOK):

"Reader's Roundup," *Iron Man*, Vol. 28, No.1, Oct/Nov, 1968, p 42. Peary Rader sketches out the "Kelso" or Lat shrug for his readers in the first mention of the author's work in print.

"The Kelso Shrug Course" and "The Bone Structure And Growth Course" copyrighted 1981. *These are genuine, registered copyrights.*

(TRAINING) "The Kelso Shrug System", *Powerlifting USA*, March, 1984.

"Variations of the Shrug Principle," *American Fitness Quarterly*, April, 1985.

"Shrug Variations for Bodybuilders," *Iron Man*, January, 1986, p 52.

"ZAP THE TRAPS," *Iron Man*, July, 1988.

"A Shrugger'sGuide," *Muscular Development*, January, 1989, p 45.

"Using the Trap Bar," *Powerlifting USA*, April, 1989, p 15.

"The Kelso Shrug Revisited," *Powerlifting USA*, September, 1989, p 40.

"Shrug Variations for Bodybuilders and Powerlifters," *Iron Man*, Dec, 1989.

"The Kelso File," *Hardgainer*, November, 1990, p 10.

"Bone Structure and Growth I," *Hardgainer*, January, 1991, p 21.

"Bone Structure and Growth II," *Hardgainer*, March, 1991, p 28.

"Shrug Variations," *Hardgainer*, January, 1993, p 24.

"The Kelso Shrug System," *Powerlifting USA*, June 1993, p 24.

"The Trap Bar – The New Basic," *Hardgainer*, July-August, 1993, p 30.

The gang from Matsumoto Gym in Utsunomiya, home to many of Japan's best powerlifters and body-builders. The author is top row, second from left. Hiroo Matsumoto, owner, lower right.

Mike Bucci of Phoenix, Arizona, demonstrates the "Margarita Shrug." He and Pat Henley, honchos of the Iron Jungle training clubs, invented this "exercise."

The author with three-time USA Olympic weightlifting team coach Jim Schmitz, at Jim's Valencia Street Fitness Center in San Francisco. March, 2002.

GLOSSARY

(The following glossary is comprised of some of the most frequently mentioned terms used in this book. Most are in common use in the weight-training field).

Abs — Abdominal muscles. Cover the "stomach" from sternum to crotch.

Assistance exercise — Movements designed to aid and develop performance of a specific competitive lift. Example: Close grip bench press for tricep and anterior deltoid power for the bench press.

Bench Press — One of the three lifts contested in powerlifting. Performed by lying on a flat bench and pressing the bar to arms' length from the chest. An unparalled upper-body developer.

Bench Shrug — Raising and lowering the bar by adducting and retracting the scapulae (shoulder blades) while arms are kept straight. Performed in bench press position.

Bent-over rowing — Performed standing while bent forward from the waist. Bar is pulled up to the chest or abdomen from arms' length, with a variety of hand grips and spacings.

Bent-over-shrugs — Done in bent-over row position. Bar raised by retraction of the scapula with straight arms. Handgrip and spacing varies.

Bone structure — Refers to proportion, length, and thickness of bones, and their relationship to each other, which in turn affects leverage and potential for carrying muscle mass.

Cable cross over machine shrug — Weights are pulled in from the side by scapular retraction. Straight arms.

Clean and jerk — One of the two competitive lifts in weightlifting. Called the King of Lifts, the bar is first lifted from the floor to the shoulders in one movement. The lifter then stands erect and thrusts the bar to lockout overhead by using the arms and legs.

Christmas tree — Advanced development of the lower edges of the lat muscles as they run toward the spine, making a shape looking like the bottom of a Christmas tree.

Conventional shrug — See standing shrug.

Deadlift — One of the three lifts contested in powerlifting. Perhaps the most demanding exercise of all. One merely stands up with the bar with straight arms. A stiff leg deadlift is performed by bending at the waist and lifting without using the legs.

Erectors — Muscles of the lower back that parallel the spine.

Finding the groove — The path of the bar during a competitive lift. Every lifter must practice until he finds the combination of bar path and body movement that allows him to lift most efficiently.

Flies — Exercises with dumb bells performed with straight or bent arms on a flat or inclined bench. Useful for chest box expansion and pectoral development. DBs are lowered out to the side and returned to a position over the chest.

Gerard Trap Bar — Specialty bar for heavy back and leg training. Increases efficiency of the exercises while reducing lower back stress.

Gironda-style dips — The late Vince Gironda, the Iron Guru, taught a lean-forward, knees-up, elbows-out style for isolating the pectorals when performing parallel bar dips for bodybuilding training. This book suggests a more balanced position.

Hise breathing shrug — Holding a bar across the shoulders and shrugging it up while doing exaggerating breathing. Named for Joe Hise, the famous bulk pioneer.

Holds — Retracting the scapulae and holding, often for a count of four, in order to get maximum benefit. See chapters three and four. Can be used statically, contracted or not, at any stage of any lift, positive or negative.

Kelso Shrugs — A training principle for developing the entire shoulder girdle through variations of adduction and retraction of the scapulae.

Kelso Shrug, The – Bent over (or face down on an inclined bench) shrugs using a variety of hand grips and spacings. Over or under grips are used. The "Kelso" specifically is with an underhand or curl grip with emphasis on the lats and lower traps during the contraction.

Lat Flair — An older bodybuilders' posing term, referring to a back-viewed lat spread in which the scapulae are semi-dislocated for extra width. A "muscle control" trick. See the cable crossover shrug and wide grip shrug.

Lateral Arch — In competition bench pressing, jamming the shoulder blades together and down against the bench so that the sternum is raised. This position is usually held throughout the lift.

Lats — The latissimus dorsi muscles, which give the back its V-shape. They pull the arms down and back, and aid in pulling shoulders to the rear. Very important to the deadlift and the bench press.

Lat Shrug — *See Kelso Shrug above.*

Lat spread — A standard bodybuilding pose seen from the front. The lats are "spread" by rotating the scapulae out to the side (the V shape).

Lockout — Usually refers to straightening the arms in the last 1/3 or 1/4 of a pressing movement. Many set the bar to various heights in a rack to hit this range.

Max — The top poundage possible for one repetition in any movement. To "max out" is to test one's ability in a one-repetition lift. The author advises against maxing out regularly, but rather recommends using cycling or periodization regimes leading to a max attempt.

Negative Shrugs — Mirror-image movements that resist the weight as it returns to the starting position or moves away from the contracted position.

Olympic lifter — Common usage, technically incorrect, for "weightlifter." One who competes in the snatch and clean and jerk or "Olympic" style. Subject to change, as powerlifting has long been competed in the World Games, which are now (as of August 2001) under the patronage of the International Olympic Committee.

Overhead shrug — Shrugging while holding the weight overhead. Practiced by "Olympic" weightlifters.

Pecs — Gym slang for the pectoral muscles across the chest.

Power Clean — Exercise pulling the bar from floor or knee height to pressing or jerking position at the shoulder. When bar reaches maximum height, the elbows are whipped under the bar and forward to rack the bar at the shoulder.

Powerlifter — One who competes in the squat, bench press, and deadlift.

Power shrug — Done by setting up like a weightlifter and pulling the bar upward, continuing the upward path of the bar by shrugging toward the ears without bending the arms.

Pre-exhaustion technique — Developed by Robert Kennedy of *Muscle Mag International*, Art Jones, and others. One uses a single joint exercise before a multi-joint movement to allow full fatigue of the targeted muscle group to be reached quickly.

Pullover — Chest expansion movement, usually performed on a flat bench with straight arms. Weight is lowered behind the head while inhaling.

Range of motion — Full extension and recovery from start to finish of any exercise. May be varied according to trainee's purpose.

Rear Deltoid — Muscle group at outside rear of shoulder. Actively engaged in any pulling movement using the arms.

Rearward Shrug — Non-specific term used by some writers to refer to bent over or inclined bench shrugs, lat shrugs, "Kelso" shrugs, and so forth.

Repetition — The performance of an exercise movement or lift one time.

Retraction of scapulae — The shrugging motion. Rotating the scapulae toward each other in any direction so as to achieve muscular contraction.

Rhomboid — Extremely powerful but little appreciated muscles of the upper back that act to pull the shoulders back and aid in any pulling motion.

Scapulae (scapula, singular) — The shoulder blades. Large mobile bones of the upper back to which many muscles are attached.

Serratus shrug — Incorrect name for Bench Shrug.

Shrug — Common name for standing upright with a bar or dumbbells at arms' length and trying to touch the ears with the shoulders. In this book, it is the movement of the scapulae to the rear, forward, up, or down to a contraction of various muscle groups.

Shrug dip — Performed in same position as parallel bar dips. Also known as Monkey Dips. Carves out the lats, pecs, and serratus.

Shrug row — Using a short pull with the arms at the most stressful point of a shrug movement to enhance muscular contraction.

Snatch — One of the two competitive lifts in weightlifting. The bar is lifted from the floor and locked out overhead in one continuous motion.

Spotter — Person or persons attending a powerlifter or trainee who prevent the bar from injuring the lifter if he fails in his attempt.

Spring Set Shrug — Holding a spring set (chest expander) behind the back and pressing the arms straight out to the side, and then using scapular motion to extend and retract the cables. A lat spread under positive and negative tension.

Squat — One of the three lifts contested in powerlifting. Often said to be the best exercise of all for gaining strength and overall size. Variations include the power squat, high bar, bar held in front, the "Hack" squat (for old-time wrestler George Hackenschmidt) and others. By carrying the bar across the shoulders and simply lowering the body by bending the knees while the torso is kept erect, over half the muscles of the body are engaged. Chest expansion results from accompanying heavy breathing. Different areas of the thighs (and hips) are engaged depending on the style used.

Standing Shrug — Standard or standing shrug where a weight hanging from arms' length is raised up toward the ears without bending the elbows.

Sternum — Breastbone in center of chest, the bone to which the ribs are attached.

Teres muscle — Another of several small muscles of the upper back that aid in scapular movement.

Trapezius — Very powerful muscle group on either side of the spine, extending from the base of the skull out to the deltoids and down to the middle of the upper back. Engaged in any pulling movement, especially those that raise the bar vertically.

USAPL — Powerlifting federation that is America's affiliate in the International Powerlifting Federation, which is connected to the Olympics through the World Games. A large number of competing federations exist, almost all in the USA, because of differences over rules, drug testing, and equipment.

Walkouts — Taking the bar out of the uprights, backing out and setting up as if to squat, but with more weight than you can full squat. Some do a ¼ squat before racking.

Printed in the United States
1258200002B/47-48

9 781587 361166